# THE RESURRECTION OF ENGLISH EDUCATION

Dr. Daehui Peter Lee

# THE RESURRECTION OF ENGLISH EDUCATION

First Edition

*The fear of the Lord is the beginning of wisdom and the knowledge of the Holy Spirit is understanding (Proverbs 9:10).*

Lee, Daehui Peter

ISBN 978-89-98636-04-3

Published by Hanol Publisher

Hanol Bldg. 3rd floor, 133-3 Seongsan-dong, Mapo-gu, Seoul, Korea

Tel: 376-4298, 376-4295~7

Fax: 302-8073

http://www.hanol.co.kr

E-mail: hanol@hanol.co.kr



Lee, Daehui Peter

The Resurrection of English Education: The ultimate guide to successful methods for listening, speaking, reading, and writing in English / Daehui Peter Lee, first edition.

Hanol Publisher

Printed in Korea

# Preface

Why do you want to learn the English language? This is a very simple question which may be asked of all English learners. Even though it is a very simple question, there may not be many people who could properly give an answer. Do you have a specific aim or purpose in learning English? Please think about your own answer on the importance of learning English. If you don't know the answer to this question, you must think about it first, and then, decide your specific aim and purpose for learning English.

Many students have learned English since kindergarten or elementary school. Many parents hope that their children speak English well. There are many cutting-edge techniques and equipment which can help students learn English efficiently and effectively. The number of English institutes has dramatically increased in a decade. Job applicants have to prepare for English interviews because speaking English is a basic qualification in order to obtain a job position. All these phenomena indicate the importance of English proficiency in our society. Thus, many people struggle to learn English because they feel they will benefit a lot from this knowledge. However, it is hard to discover someone who can speak English really well.

What seems to be the problem? Why do English learners fail to speak English even if they have learned English for more than ten years? Why do English learners fail to speak good English even if they have been exposed to many cutting edge English educational techniques and equipment?

This book *The Resurrection of English Education* hopes to teach and guide you into the CORRECT method of learning English. You may doubt the correct method of learning English which is explained in this book. However, you actually know the correct method of learning English because you have already learned your native language and mastered it. If you want to know the correct method of learning English, please open this book and discover the secrets of learning English. If you say to yourself that you have given up learning English for several years, please think differently this time: "I have paused for several years in learning English and now is the time to start anew!" Please think about your potential and take up the challenge in learning English. As you know, there are many benefits to English proficiency, so it is worthwhile and meritorious for you to learn English according to the valuable explanations and suggestions contained in this book.

Remember that every human being has a talent for language! But the problem is not you or the learner, but the incorrect method of learning English that you have followed, one without specific aims or purposes. Please don't read this book if your focus is only on English scores without real English fluency. This book is a guide for someone who wants to listen, speak, read, and write English well.

I hope that you will have a wonderful journey through this book in discovering not only the correct method of learning English, but also your language potential, all of which can make your dreams come true.

Daehui Peter Lee

# Acknowledgments

Thank God, Jesus Christ, and the Holy Spirit for completing this book. Jesus Christ is the light of my life.

In the beginning was the Word, and the Word was with God, and the Word was God. He was in the beginning with God. All things were made through Him, and without Him nothing was made that was made. In Him was life, and the life was the light of men.

John 1: 1-4

I hope this book becomes a light to shine the right path for all English learners. In the name of Jesus Christ my Lord, Amen!

# Table of Contents

# PART ONE

## WADING THROUGH THE DARKNESS IN LEARNING ENGLISH

# 1

## Do you think that you have been running in the right or wrong direction in learning the English language?

"Learning English is difficult."

"I am not good at learning English."

"I gave up learning English because I have no talent for English."

"I feel stressed when learning English because there are too many words that I have to memorize."

"I have studied English for more than ten years since elementary school. However, I cannot speak English. I don't know why."

"What is the problem in learning English?"

Many people have similar opinions to those above when it comes to learning English. They generally dedicate their time and effort to learning English. They hope to speak English well, and expect that their English ability can help them obtain a good job. They believe that English is one of the most well-known languages in the world. They also believe that fluency in English is highly beneficial for engaging in domestic and international business. Thus, they study English hard and believe that they will eventually become good English speakers.

However, they think that learning English is difficult. The more serious problem is that they give up learning English because they think that they don't have any talent for English.

This is totally wrong!

Do you think that someone can be talented in English and someone else can be less talented? No way! This is absolutely not true. English is a language and languages are spoken by every human being. Giving up learning English because of the lack of talent is not a correct idea. If you give up learning English because you are not patient, that is also the wrong attitude. Although, of course, some people can make a strong decision to learn English, but later give up after one or two months. This is the case of an impatient person.

However, if you really want to discover the real problem in learning English, you must think about the role of a language first. The following question is a very simple one, so please give an answer.

WHY DO YOU WANT TO LEARN ENGLISH?

Let's suppose there are two answers to the question above. Which one would you choose?

First Answer: I want to learn English because I need a high

score on English examinations.

Second Answer: I want to learn English because I want to listen, speak, read, and write English well.

Which one did you choose? Unfortunately, many people choose the first answer instead of the second one, even though they know that the second answer is much better. People may say that they need high scores on English examinations because schools and companies demand excellent scores. People also think that there is no option for them because they need high scores on English examinations in order to get a job or enter a university.

Getting high scores is absolutely a good motivation for English learners. However, what if you have been running in the wrong direction in learning English? What if you could not speak English well even if you had already been learning English for more than ten years? What if you could not listen, speak, read, and write English well, even though you have high scores on English examinations? What if you could not speak English well even though you are knowledgeable about English grammar?

You must know the fact that English is nothing more than a language. It means that there are specific steps in learning English. Learning English is not the same as learning other academic subjects such as mathematics, chemistry, philosophy, and so on. English must be learned in a NATURAL WAY. The natural way is the manner by which you learned your mother tongue.

This book is composed of many dialogues and discussions in order to discover how to learn English and practice it. Through a lot of discussions and arguments, Dr. Peter Lee and his students are wading through the darkness in order to discover the correct way of learning English. You may become one of the students who discuss various topics about learning English.

Please open the door and get in the class in order to start digging up the ground in which the secret method of learning English is buried. The class starts now!

Dr. Peter Lee: Hi, everyone! I am glad to meet all of you here in this class. My name is Daehui Peter Lee and I will be teaching you English this semester. I would like to start this class by asking the following question: *Do you think that the way you are learning English is correct?*

Somang Kim: What does that question mean, Dr. Lee? Are you asking me whether the way I am learning English now is correct or incorrect?

Dr. Peter Lee: Yes, you are right. What do you think?

Somang Kim: Actually, I have not thought about that. I have not thought whether the way I have been learning English is correct or not. Usually, students learn English starting in elementary school. This includes lessons on vocabulary, grammar, conversational fluency, and many other topics.

Dr. Peter Lee: Would you please share with us the way you have learned English?

Somang Kim: Sure, Dr. Lee! I remember that I learned English since middle school. First, I memorized English vocabulary that might be useful for middle school students. It was an obligation that I had to memorize twenty English words every day. Actually, my mother forced me to memorize them. If I didn't, my mother hit me with a stick.

Dr. Peter Lee: Oh, I feel sorry about that. I think that it would be pretty hard for you to memorize English vocabulary every day. Is that right?

Somang Kim: Yes, I thought that it was really hard for me to memorize English vocabulary every day. Maybe other students feel the same way.

Dr. Peter Lee: I think so. Would you please tell me why it is so hard?

Somang Kim: Memorizing twenty English words every day was pretty hard for me because I had not learned English much when I was in elementary school. For example, I memorized twenty English words every day per week, and after six or seven days I could memorize one hundred forty English words. It is easy to calculate, right? Twenty times seven equals one hundred forty.

Dr. Peter Lee: Were you able to memorize all the one hundred forty words each week?

Somang Kim: No. This is because my memory didn't follow the simply way I calculated the number of words each week. I think that no one can actually remember every word memorized. It would be impossible for human beings to memorize all of the English vocabulary they encounter each day.

Dr. Peter Lee: But I would like to know something, Somang. Why do you want to memorize all of this English vocabulary? Is there someone pushing you to do this?

Somang Kim: Actually, no one. Nobody is pushing me to memorize all of this English vocabulary. I just like it because I believe that the more English words I know, the better I can use English.

Dr. Peter Lee: You know, Somang. You may be right. If you know more English words, then you can make many English phrases and sentences when talking or writing in English. If you knew more English vocabulary, then you could understand and express yourself in English better. However, when talking or writing in English, do you use all of the English words that you studied before?

Somang Kim: No, but many students think that it's right to know more English words in order to understand English better. That knowledge in English would also be helpful in getting good scores during English examinations.

Dr. Peter Lee: You are right. Many students want to have good scores on English examinations. But they usually focus only on English examinations. That inclination is perilous indeed. I am going to explain later on why it is risky, and not a good idea if you only focus on getting high scores on English examinations.

Somang Kim: That would be great, Dr. Lee. I would like to learn why it is not good to just focus on getting high scores in English examinations.

Dr. Peter Lee: Yes, Somang, but that will be a bit later. For now, I would like to focus on the word believe in your statement. I really like the word believe because the word can make people feel confident and secure. Therefore, I think it is a nice word. Then, I would like to ask another question - do you believe that the way you have chosen and followed to learn English is correct? This is such an important question in learning English. For example, if you believe that the way you learned English is correct, then you may continue to study and learn English in that way. I also think that you may already be very confident and not skeptical in learning English because you are learning English the best way you can.

Somang Kim: Actually, Dr. Lee, I am not sure if the way that I have been learning English since middle school is correct. I don't think that I am learning English in a perfect manner, but at the same time, I cannot figure out exactly what is the problem!

Dr. Peter Lee: Can you clarify your answer, Somang?

Somang Kim: Actually, Dr. Lee, I think I have a headache all of a sudden, since you asked me that question on my way in learning English. I have never thought about whether my English-learning method is right or wrong. I think that everyone is memorizing English words all the time. It is a general phenomenon. That is not wrong as far as I am concerned. It may not exactly be the most correct or efficient way, but I think it could be one good way to learn English. Thus, I believe that memorizing words is one good way to learn English.

Dr. Peter Lee: I know what you mean, Somang. However, I would like to teach you what the right steps for learning English are.

Somang Kim: That will be interesting, Dr. Lee. I really would like to know the right steps for learning English.

Dr. Peter Lee: I am glad to share with you my knowledge about the matter. As you know, many students are fond of memorizing English vocabulary. They also believe that it is the right way to learn English. However, why do they stop learning English and even give up learning English all of sudden? Why do they think that they don't have a talent for learning English? Why do they think that they have to go to the United States, the United Kingdom, Canada, and other English countries to learn English?

Somang Kim: Your questions make me think, Dr. Lee.

Dr. Peter Lee: And here's more: Do they believe that living in English countries is a good way to learn English? Why do Korean parents strive to send their children to English-speaking countries for learning English? Do they believe that learning English in English-speaking countries might be much better than learning English in Korea? If this is true, then all students who learn English should go to English-speaking countries. If this is true, students who are learning English in English-speaking countries should be much better English users than ones who are learning English in Korea. Do you think that is right? Do you think that an English environment is enormously important for students who are learning English? There are tens of thousands of questions related to learning English. That is why I am asking you whether the way you learn English is correct or incorrect.

Somang Kim: After I heard you list those questions, I am not even sure now if that way of learning English is right or wrong.

Dr. Peter Lee: Have you ever been to a hospital when you were sick?

Somang Kim: Of course. Doctors usually ask me many questions and explain to me why I am sick. Later, they write a list of medicines I am supposed to take to be cured or healed from my ailment. I trust the prescription that they write for me and I give it to a pharmacist in order to receive the medicine.

Dr. Peter Lee: I am using exactly the same method that doctors have done for you. Although I am not a doctor in a hospital, I am kind of a doctor wanting to heal all of the students in this class who have similar problems in learning English.

Somang Kim: That is great, Dr. Lee. I really need some help from you.

Dr. Peter Lee: Okay, do you know what PBL is? What does it stand for?

Somang Kim: I don't know.

Dr. Peter Lee: PBL stands for Problem-Based Learning. This is a method in learning to find out a solution to a problem or difficult situation by collaborating and cooperating with group members. You are discussing intricate problems and issues in order to get the right answer. Do you want to try it?

Students: Yes, we do. We want to try it out.

Dr. Peter Lee: Okay, then, let's do it! All of the students in this class, please come up to the front and write down one of your favorite or recommended ways to learn English on this blackboard. Please come up now and let us know your particular way of learning English. Let us know and share what your favorite way of learning English is. Please write down only ONE effective and efficient way in learning English.

The methods written by students on the blackboard on how to learn English show the following information:

1. *Watching English movies*
2. *Meeting English native speakers*
3. *Studying English grammar*
4. *Memorizing and repeating English vocabulary*
5. *Memorizing all the sentences written in English textbooks*
6. *Watching English dramas*
7. *Watching English news*
8. *Using a telephone to converse with native speakers in English*
9. *Attending English language training programs in English countries*
10. *Participating in internship programs in English countries*
11. *Participating in working holiday programs in English countries*
12. *Taking private lessons from English native speakers*
13. *Reading English textbooks and newspapers*
14. *Making foreign friends who come from English countries*

15. *Reading English materials aloud every day*

16. *Listening to and singing English songs*

17. *Using an English-Korean dictionary*

18. *Writing e-mails to a pen pal in English*

19. *Talking to each other in English*

Dr. Peter Lee: Thank you very much for sharing your English learning methods. These are interesting methods that you suggest. Probably, there could be more useful ways to learn English. But I don't want to judge which one is good and bad, but to try to evaluate the method that you recommend, because we have to analyze whether these would be effective and efficient ways to produce positive results. Now, let's discuss, one at a time, your recommended methods for learning English.

# 2

## Various topics for discussion in learning English

### Discussion topic 1: Watching English movies

Dr. Peter Lee: First, Somang suggested that watching English movies is a good way to learn English. What do other students think about this method? Is it good or bad?

Yonggi Lee: I think that watching English movies is useful and helpful. There are many kinds of English movies. For example, action movies, romance, animation, science fiction, mystery, suspense, and so on. There are tens of thousands of English movies from which we can select our favorite one. We can enjoy it, and at the same time get familiar with some new English words.

Sarang Park: I definitely agree with Yonggi's opinion. Watching movies is an effective way for us to learn English. Even if I haven't been to English-speaking countries such as the United States or Canada, I can understand Westerners' lifestyles from movies. Of course, it would be hard to say that actors or actresses in those movies behave in exactly the same way as real people do in different societies. However, I can understand their various lifestyles from movies. In addition, there are many useful expressions that I can use in talking to people when I am in similar situations in real life.

Dr. Peter Lee: Yes, I agree with you. You are correct in saying that watching movies is extremely helpful and useful for learning English. You can also practice some expressions that you remember from all these movies. Then, what movies are useful for students here? Would you recommend your favorite movie for helping us to learn English?

Sarang Park: I think that there are several movies which are helpful. I cannot exactly say the titles of these movies because all the students here have different preferences. I just want to tell you about one important thing. I usually watch movies which include many conversations rather than actions. In the case of action movies, there is much less dialogue, thus less chance of familiarizing myself with English conversations. In romance movies, there are many conversations and discussions similar to the ones we usually hear from Korean movies; that is why I prefer romance movies rather than action movies.

Dr. Peter Lee: Sarang, that is good advice! But I am wondering whether watching movies is a good starting point for English learners. The length of a movie is normally one and a half hours and, sometimes, conversations between actors and actresses are so fast for beginners to understand. What do you think about that?

Sarang Park: Yes, you are right. I could understand English movies without subtitles after I developed my English level to intermediate. If I were a beginner in learning English, watching movies would not be a good way for me to learn English. Without subtitles, I would probably not understand what people in those movies are talking about. But some specific movies made for elementary school students can be helpful for beginners to learn English. Do you think this is correct?

Dr. Peter Lee: I am not really sure if movies intended for kids can be helpful for adult learners, even though their English proficiency is not high. For example, I am more than thirty years old already and if I watched movies made for kids, I would be bored because the same or similar sentences are repeated over and over. What I mean to say is that the movies for kindergarten or elementary school kids may be quite easy for adults. But movies for upper levels of elementary school students could be useful for beginners in learning English. Selecting movies or films suitable to one's level of English ability is quite important for beginners. We are going to discuss this more when we are on the topic of setting an individual strategy.

## Discussion topic 2: Meeting English native speakers

Dr. Peter Lee: This time around, let us talk about another method in learning English. Boram suggests that meeting English native speakers is also helpful for English learners. What do you think about that? Is it a good method? Is there anyone who has a similar opinion to Boram's? Would you explain it by sharing more details?

Miso Han: I totally agree with his opinions because I have experienced this myself. Talking with English native speakers is good practice for me to learn English. Sometimes, English native speakers correct my sentences so that I can learn how to make grammatically correct sentences. Correcting the sentences and expressions that I use while we are conversing can be bothersome to some native English speakers. However, most of them don't mind because we are good friends. Most of them are just generous enough to help me learn the English language, and they know and understand why I am trying to use English for a conversation with them.

My friends like that fact that I am very friendly, gregarious, and sociable. I think that nobody can really make perfect English sentences all the time, especially, when one is starting to learn English. I started speaking English when I was a kid. I was very interested in expressing my feeling and opinions in English in front of English native speakers. They actually understood what I meant to say even though my sentences were incorrect.

Sometimes, we misunderstood each other but we kept talking to each other. Eventually, we understood each other's feelings and opinions perfectly.

Dr. Peter Lee: Oh, that is very interesting, Miso. Would you please tell us more? In particular, why did you and the native speakers misunderstand each other? Can you share some particular reasons? How did it happen?

Miso Han: I am not exactly sure about that. But I think that there are several possible reasons.

First, I could not explain what I meant to say to him one hundred percent in English. I was learning English and even though English native speakers knew the fact that I was practicing English, they misinterpreted my words and sometimes understood them in a completely different way. But this is actually not surprising as it happens to others. This is a similar phenomenon when Koreans talk to each other in Korean, but misunderstandings happen because of the speakers' different ways of perception or comprehension. Basically, men and women have a different mindset; that is, men typically behave differently than women. Cultural differences also might cause disparate perceptions and understanding.

Dr. Peter Lee: I see what you mean. You are actually telling us more complicated issues about human beings. Languages are very important to understand each other but different cultural perspectives are also significant for all language learners. Do you agree with this?

Miso Han: Yes. I totally agree. However, there is one more thing I want to comment on.

In the past, my foreign friends and I talked to each other in English and we realized that some misleading statements were contained in our conversations. However, we finally understood each other because we realized that all the complicated problems might be solved by our conversations.

Then, my foreign friends encouraged me and kept telling me that I was good at talking in English, even though they noticed some mistakes. However, the more I talked to them in English, the fewer incorrect sentences I formed. Of course, I still could not avoid some mistakes in English because, basically, I am not really a native English speaker. However, I will keep on talking to them in English because I am sure that someday, I can make perfect sentences to avoid any misunderstanding between us. After all, PRACTICE MAKES PERFECT!

And I believe that I can further reduce mistaken sentences as I talk more and more. I actually don't want to stop learning English. I want to keep walking on this journey. Someday, I am sure I can use English very well and I believe that that day is coming fast. And why do I feel this way? It is because I am making my best effort to learn the English language.

Dr. Peter Lee: Great! That is such a beautiful thought that students here must learn and remember. Have you ever thought about how long you have to learn English if you want to use English well?

Of course it depends on what levels of English proficiency you hope to acquire in the future. But I do know and am sure that it would be impossible for you to completely finish learning English in a short period of time. I mean, some authors claim that after three to six months you can completely understand English and you can finish learning English within one year. I am sorry but I don't think so.

From my personal experience, I am sure that those estimates are absolutely inaccurate. How could human beings finish learning foreign languages in about a year? If there is someone who can say that all the four communication competencies, listening, speaking, reading, and writing, can be mastered in a year, that person is definitely a genius! I am not a genius so I would be totally impressed by someone who needs only a year to master a foreign language.

I usually meet people who are "average." Their intelligence quotients are less than 160. Admittedly, my intelligence quotient is just over a hundred. That is why I am suggesting that the amount of time required for learning English is about two or three years.

Don't misunderstand me, please! I say that two to three years is a normal period for "average" people to learn and use a foreign language effectively. I am telling all of you here about this because later on, you will make a specific plan for learning English. I will be guiding you on how to make that plan as well as how many years you need in order to reach the levels you aim for.

Anyway, from this discussion, we learned that talking to English native speakers can be helpful for English learners.

## Discussion topic 3: Studying English grammar

Dr. Peter Lee: The next recommendation written on the board is about studying English grammar. What do you think about that? Do you think that studying English grammar can be helpful for English learners? If you agree with that opinion, please tell us why you think so; and if you disagree with that opinion, please explain why you think otherwise? Is there anyone who can share?

Innae Jeong: Well, I disagree with the suggestion that studying English grammar is helpful or useful. At the same time, it would also be hard to say that studying English grammar is absolutely and completely unhelpful. Rather, I am neutral, neither totally agreeing nor totally disagreeing.

I strongly insist, however, that teaching English in a grammar-centric way must be changed. In English classes, I got very tired while learning some specific grammar terms, namely: present perfect, present participle, past participle, gerund, to-infinitive, conjunctions, and prepositions.

In grammar, there are too many terms to memorize and it is too difficult for me to comprehend. I never learned Korean grammar while learning Korean. I don't know why I have to spend so much time in learning about English grammar in English classes. Would you please give us advice about this and at the same time, explain whether English grammar is necessarily needed for one who is learning English?

Dr. Peter Lee: I would be more than glad to explain it to you all.

In order to explain it to you clearly, it would be better for you to understand why English grammar has been commonly regarded as an important measuring tool in Korea. English grammar examinations can help English teachers to evaluate English abilities with ease. From the 1960s to the 1990s, the number of students in one class was more than fifty, so that it was not easy for English teachers to examine every aspect of the students' English communicative competencies, such as listening, speaking, reading, and writing. Thus, English grammar became one of the most straightforward measuring tools for English teachers to assess the performance or learning levels of students. Students, then, just tried to find out the correct answers to questions pertinent to English grammar. Perhaps, they never thought about why they had to learn English grammar. Students who knew and memorized all the unnecessary information about English grammar written in English grammar textbooks were regarded as English grammar geniuses or grammarians. At that time, students didn't consider listening, speaking, and even writing in English. They just focused on English grammar and reading sections.

Innae Jeong: Even up to now, students are still learning English grammar in school or private institutes. They are always preparing for English grammar examinations and they still think that they are good at English if they know English grammar better than others. Actually, if someone gets high scores in English grammar examinations compared with other students, it simply means that he is better than others only in the case of English grammar. Is my assumption correct?

Dr. Peter Lee: Hmm…, let me see… I think it would be difficult to say that a student is good in English if he is good in English grammar. I think that there is another way to explain this question.

I taught a kid who was about twelve years old. We talked to each other in English and he was very good at English listening and speaking. I did know that he was good in English reading and writing or not. I tested him by using some English questions related to English grammar retrieved from previous TOEIC examinations. Many students in this class now may think that the kid might not figure out any correct answers to the questions given. However, he knew all the correct answers to the questions that I gave. I was amazed by his English knowledge. Actually, I was shocked. I asked myself how he could know all the right answers even though he has never studied formal English grammar.

I asked him about his reasons for selecting those answers and he said, "I think that it is the right answer, but I cannot explain why it is the answer. I just feel it. Am I wrong?"

Innae Jeong: And how did you respond to his question, sir?

Dr. Peter Lee: I said nothing. I really said nothing… but I think that his answer might be correct. Do you know why?

In order to help you to understand why, I want to ask you about the following question first. Have you ever thought of Korean grammar while talking to people around you, in Korean?

Innae Jeong: No. There is nobody who thinks about Korean grammar first before saying the words in Korean. This is because we are Koreans and talking comes naturally.

Dr. Peter Lee: That is not an issue here! We are not focused on matters like you are speaking Korean because you are Korean. I am simply asking you about a basic question, "Have you ever thought about Korean grammar whenever you talk to Korean people in Korean?"

Innae Jeong: Never! I never think of Korean grammar before I speak Korean to other Koreans. There is no one who thinks about Korean grammar when he speaks Korean. In the case of writing Korean sentences, such as essays or professional papers, I usually consider the structure and flow of sentences and not Korean grammar. I think that better structured sentences may be more readable and understandable.

Dr. Peter Lee: If you are talking about writing issues, that is different from what I meant to say. Sometimes, grammatical knowledge is definitely helpful for writers to make sentences accurate and professional. My question is, whether you are thinking about Korean grammar or not when you are TALKING to people in Korean.

Innae Jeong: No! I said "no" already. Why do you keep asking me this question?

Dr. Peter Lee: I keep asking you about that question because this is a very important query for everyone who wants to learn English. Many students still believe that English grammar is necessary to enhance their English proficiency, even though it is not true. There are many possible reasons that students have the same opinion.

First, many English examinations are related to English grammar. If you look at the questions on elementary, middle school, high school English examinations, it is obvious that many questions are pertinent to English grammar. Many English grammatical questions are also found in college and university entrance examinations.

Innae Jeong: Why are those questions needed when entering colleges and universities? Do they think that grammatical knowledge equals English proficiency? Instead of the questions related to English grammar, there could be many other more useful questions for screening students who would like to study in colleges and universities. I mean, tests on speaking, reading, and even writing, instead of simply on grammar, could be much more valuable and relevant to select students who have better English capabilities and those who would do well in their degree programs.

Dr. Peter Lee: Thank you, Innae. You are very smart, indeed, and what you said is exactly correct. Speaking tests, reading tests, and writing tests are much more accurate methods for evaluating students' English proficiency. Normally, students who enter colleges or universities have studied English for more than six years, if they started learning English from middle school.

Innae Jeong: If they have been studying English for more than six years, how come many students still have difficulty in speaking English?

Dr. Peter Lee: Basically, because they are not confident yet with their abilities. They are just too nervous to speak in English or probably worried about what they will say next during English-speaking situations. Someone said that there is no correlation between learning English grammar and the lack of English speaking ability. Thus, it is incorrect to say that more or less knowledge of English grammar correlates with English speaking ability.

However, many students still consider the importance of English grammar while learning English. That is one of the serious problems of English education in Korea now. I usually ask this question to students. What is a gerund? Would you please tell me what a gerund is?

Innae Jeong: A gerund is a word plus *ing*.

Dr. Peter Lee: That would be a correct answer if I asked you what was the form of a gerund? But that is not my question, actually. I am asking you about the definition of a gerund. What is a gerund? Even though it is not a difficult question, students cannot answer correctly. Do you know why?

Innae Jeong: I am vague about the reason, Dr. Lee.

Dr. Peter Lee: Most students have studied a gerund and probably know various usages of a gerund. However, they could not say the basic definition of a gerund. One English-English dictionary indicates the following: “a gerund is a noun formed from a verb which refers to an action, process, or state.” I think this definition is already enough for English learners to know what a gerund is. But Korean students learning English have to understand too much English grammar, not only a gerund but also the infinitive, uncountable nouns, countable nouns, relative clauses, auxiliary verbs and other detailed grammatical terms.

Innae Jeong: Yes, that is right. In a Korean class, learning Korean grammar is difficult for me even though I am a Korean. English is not my mother tongue, thus, I have even more difficulty because I am not a native English speaker. I also have to understand much more English grammar. Sometimes, I feel it is just nonsense.

Dr. Peter Lee: I also think that memorizing too much English grammar is nonsense. But many people do it without questioning. I don’t know why they keep on doing it. Thus, it would be good to discuss controversial issues related to English education before learning the language in order to find out the right pathway to learn English.

Innae Jeong: What way or ways would you recommend to us to better learn the English language?

Dr. Peter Lee: I would like to recommend that you have to think deeply about what you are learning and why you are learning it. If you don't know the relationship between what you are learning and why you are learning it, your knowledge and skills obtained from long-term training would definitely be useless. Even though you memorize a lot of English grammar while studying and learning the language, you are never going to use many such grammatical terms during the rest of your life. Many students are learning and studying English grammar without thinking carefully about the usage of English grammar.

Innae Jeong: Have you done the same, Dr. Lee, when you were much younger?

Dr. Peter Lee: Oh, yes! Actually, I did the same and I really regret it... But I gave up that method focused on English grammar and it has made a lot of difference in my journey to learning the language. If you learn something, you have to think about how to use it. This is a genuine learning process. I am not talking about whether learning English grammar is not important. I am emphasizing that too much studying of English grammar may not be useful for English learners.

Innae Jeong: Is that always true, Dr. Lee?

Dr. Peter Lee: No, because the issue related to English

grammar that we are discussing may be highly debatable. And many English teachers and learners have opinions different from mine. I really cannot force them to think the way I do. But I would like to share the following experience.

I would definitely say that I could have used my time in a more productive way if I listened to English speakers or read English materials. I would like to think that I wasted my time analyzing grammatical structures of English sentences in order to pick the right answers out of four multiple-choice options in English grammar examinations. This is simply senseless!

Innae Jeong: When, then, is studying English grammar useful?

Dr. Peter Lee: That is a good question. If you want to be a linguistic scholar in English, then, you need to examine and analyze patterns of English use. Which came first: English or English grammar?

Innae Jeong: Of course, English absolutely came first, then English grammar.

Dr. Peter Lee: Why do you think so?

Innae Jeong: I think that English grammar is the set of rules governing the structure of composed sentences. There are regular or irregular patterns and those patterns have been examined by language scholars.

Dr. Peter Lee: That is correct. Just like what you said, English grammar is the set of rules used in composing sentences in a particular way. Separate and individual parts are gathered together revealing similar or different patterns and forms.

Innae Jeong: What are those patterns and forms?

Dr. Peter Lee: Those patterns and forms are the structure of a language. But don't worry! This is the kind of knowledge that you need not know now because the patterns are too elaborate for you to understand. Let us talk about the next topic.

## Discussion topic 4: Memorizing and repeating English vocabulary

Dr. Peter Lee: Do you think that memorizing and repeating English vocabulary every day is a good method to learn English?

Dajim Choi: I think that English vocabulary is important to initially learn about English; memorizing English vocabulary is the most important thing that I have to do for that language.

Dr. Peter Lee: It is also an interesting topic. Do you memorize English vocabulary every day? How do you memorize English vocabulary every day?

Dajim Choi: Usually I memorize fifty English words every day. While I am reading English textbooks, I check some essential words that I don't know. And, then, I summarize those words in a note and review them every day.

Dr. Peter Lee: That is a good idea! Many students, I suppose, do the same, right? Let us look now at a more in depth aspect of the method of memorizing English words.

I am not good at Math, but let us try to calculate how many English words you can memorize per year.

If you memorize fifty English words per day, then you could memorize one thousand five hundred English words per month. And if you memorize one thousand five hundred English words per month, then you could memorize eighteen thousand English words per year.

Dajim Choi: What are you trying to imply with this analysis,

Dr. Lee?

Dr. Peter Lee: I am trying to explain that if there are more than one hundred thousand words in English vocabulary, then, you might be memorizing more than one hundred thousand English words for five or six years. Do you think this is possible? Do you think it will work? How do you review them all over and over?

If you memorize fifty words per day, it is highly possible that the next day, you will probably NOT remember all of those words you memorized earlier. And as time goes by, you may even forget more words and, eventually give up memorizing them. What do you think about that? Do you think that memorizing English words is an effective way of learning English?

Dajim Choi: There are actually many ways to memorize English words. One of them is summarizing unknown words encountered from reading materials and reviewing and using them later on. That method is really common.

Another effective method is studying textbooks which tackle specific levels of English vocabulary.

Dr. Peter Lee: Did you succeed using those methods?

Dajim Choi: I don't know. Many of my classmates do it that way to memorize English words. Is there any other particular method that you can recommend for us on how to memorize English vocabulary?

Dr. Peter Lee: Actually, there is no specific way that I can recommend to you for memorizing English words. What about just doing the basic communicative competencies of listening, speaking, reading, and writing English? It is a normal way to memorize English vocabulary, isn't it?

Don't be disappointed that I cannot tell you the secret for how to memorize English vocabulary quickly. But let me explain further.

For example, some students wish to memorize five hundred English words in one day. Do you think that it is possible? Okay, some of you might say that it is possible. But can you use them all in the proper way while speaking and writing? Now, I hope you understand what I am talking about.

Dajim Choi: We understand your point, Dr. Lee. But can you tell us tips on learning English vocabulary?

Dr. Peter Lee: Sure! First, there are erroneous ways that one must avoid when one is learning English vocabulary. Second, many students memorize English words without checking the correct English pronunciation of words. They normally use hands to memorize English words.

Dajim Choi: Hands to memorize English words? How strange is this! Can you explain this further?

Dr. Peter Lee: Yes, hands to memorize English words... You might be interested to know what this means. It means writing down (of course, using hands!) English vocabulary in a note about ten to twenty times without pronunciation practice. And many students memorize English words with their own pronunciations, which may be incorrect.

Dajim Choi: I am curious, who ever invented the use of hands in memorizing English vocabulary?

Dr. Peter Lee: I don't know who invented the way of using hands to note down words several times without reading them aloud and even without listening to the correct pronunciations. Do you usually check the accurate pronunciation of the words that you don't know? Many Korean students, actually, memorize English vocabulary by practicing wrong English pronunciation which English native speakers never understand.

(Note: 1 good source is the website howjsay.com. You just type the word and you hear a voice pronounce it both ways – American and/or British.)

Dajim Choi: I need to know English words in order to understand English materials, not to speak English. That is why I think students don't need to check correct pronunciations.

Dr. Peter Lee: That is the biggest mistake that many English learners make while learning English! Basically, language learners must use their ears and mouth to learn English vocabulary. For example, if there is a word like school that you are studying in your English textbook, you have to check the correct pronunciation first. Why don't you try pronouncing the word school?

Dajim Choi: S~C~H~O~O~R.

Dr. Peter Lee: No, you have to pronounce the "L" sound, not the "R" sound.

Dajim Choi: But what is the difference between the L and the R sound?

Dr. Peter Lee: Oh my goodness! You don't know the different sounds of those two letters?

Dajim Choi: Nobody taught me how to pronounce the alphabet.

Dr. Peter Lee: That is the most serious problem that I have ever encountered!

Dajim Choi: Why?

Dr. Peter Lee: If somebody wants to learn foreign languages, he has to think about the function of that language. This is because different languages have their own unique sounds. People who have the same mother tongue should be able to understand each other very easily. This is the basic function of having a shared field of experience in communication through a common language.

Dajim Choi: Now, I can better understand why I cannot speak English well. I have usually concentrated on reading and interpreting the meanings of English sentences. In addition, I have never taken any English-speaking test, so checking correct pronunciation has often been ignored. Sometimes, I check the correct pronunciation using the Internet.

Dr. Peter Lee: You are better than other students who never check their English pronunciations while learning English. However, you must keep in mind the basic function of a language as well as the primary purpose of learning English. Do you know why I am emphasizing the basic function of a language and the purpose of learning English?

Dajim Choi: I don't know.

Dr. Peter Lee: Based on the purpose for learning English, the direction of learning English should be modified. For example, if you only focus on reading and understanding English materials, then, you will read English materials over and over without checking the correct pronunciation of English vocabulary. Do you think this is fine, even if it may not be the right way to learn English? What do you think?

Dajim Choi: That is absolutely the wrong way! Who wants to only read and understand English materials without speaking or pronouncing the English words correctly?

Dr. Peter Lee: But you did and other students did the same. While you are learning English, have you ever thought of talking to English native speakers? Or have you ever talked to your Korean friends in English?

Dajim Choi: No, I have discussed some grammatical issues or interpretations of English sentences but not discussed any other English speaking issue. Now, I realize what my mistake was in learning English. The right method of learning English is to use my ears, mouth, eyes, and other senses. To be honest, I have used only my eyes to read English articles and hands to write down English words in notes in order to memorize them. That is why you needed to tell us the basic function of English and the purpose of learning English, right?

Dr. Peter Lee: Correct! What is a sentence? A sentence is composed of a number of words combined, with each word having its own meaning and pronunciation. The correct pronunciation of each word must be known in order to let people know the correct meaning of a sentence. Let us look at the following sentence and read it aloud.

"*The problem of his linguistic ability results from his ignorance of the correct pronunciation.*"

Dajim Choi: The problem of his linguistic ability results from his ignorance of the correct pronunciation.

Dr. Peter Lee: Something is wrong with the way you said one word in the sentence! Many students mispronounce the word RESULT. You were pronouncing not R-E-S-U-L-T, but R-E-S-U-R-T. It seems to sound like RESORT! Okay. Let us pronounce the word RESULT once more.

Students: R-E-S-U-R-T!

Dr. Peter Lee: Do you know what you sound like? Please compare my pronunciation and your pronunciation of the word RESULT. There are some words in the English language that you have to practice pronouncing in order to understand and be familiar with the different sounds. It is about phonetics.

Dajim Choi: What is phonetics?

Dr. Peter Lee: Phonetics is the study involving the correct manner of pronouncing English words. I will talk about phonetics later, but here we have examined how important pronunciations are in learning English. If you pronounce one word RESULT in the above sentence, using your own English pronunciation which is not correct, people who are listening to you will definitely NOT understand what you mean. In the process of speaking, all your messages will not be understood in the right context because it sounds different from your real intention. The different pronunciation of just a single word (in this case, RESULT), then, gives a different meaning to the sentence. Eventually, this can result in miscommunication between two persons or among many people.

Dajim Choi: Now, I understand why you are emphasizing the correct pronunciation, which is the basic step to learn English vocabulary.

Dr. Peter Lee: You are exactly correct! The basic step to learn English vocabulary is to know its accurate pronunciations. It is hard for you to pronounce words just like native English speakers do because English is not your mother tongue. However, you have to keep practicing the basic sound of each letter so that you can pronounce English words correctly. After doing this, you have to practice reading English sentences aloud and repetitively. This method is nothing new. Most people know this already. Some people know it and they practice it when they are learning English. But there are still many people who ignore pronunciation practice even if they know how important pronunciation is. This is hard to understand. I still don't know why they have this attitude.

Dajim Choi: You are right. Actually, it is not a new approach to learning English vocabulary. I have just been thinking that checking and listening to the correct English pronunciation is not necessary. There are too many words to check while reading English materials. That would be very tiring. The process of checking the correct English pronunciation of each word is kind of time-consuming. Is it right?

Dr. Peter Lee: Yes, you are correct! Checking the correct pronunciation is a time-consuming process. BUT you have to know the correct pronunciation if you want to practice aloud the CORRECT way of saying the English words. Eliminating wrong methods of learning English is the first step in establishing the correct method of learning English. Please don't waste your valuable time for learning English in wrong ways.

In the class, I give students an assignment in which they have to memorize some dialogues. In the next class meeting, I check out whether they memorized the dialogues or not. The problem is that many students memorize the dialogues using their own incorrect pronunciation. Perhaps they spent several hours memorizing them all, but their sentences are unintelligible to native English speakers because of their incorrect pronunciation. That is why English learners should examine correct pronunciations of English vocabulary first. For them to do it correctly, they MUST practice reading it aloud. The entire process may not be easy, but believe me, it is for your own good!

Dajim Choi: Until when do I have to check the correct English pronunciations?

Dr. Peter Lee: To be honest, even now, I am still checking the correct English pronunciation of some difficult words which are used in professional fields or academic areas. However, you don't need to worry about that at this time.

In the beginning, you may frequently check the correct English pronunciation of many words. However, the frequency with which you check the correct English pronunciations will drop as you learn more correct pronunciations. After checking the right sound of each English word, you have to practice reading it aloud over and over.

Dajim Choi: Does this mean, then, that we should stop writing down English words on a note?

Dr. Peter Lee: No, not at all! Writing down an English word several times on a note may also be good for helping you to remember. I don't want to prevent you from doing what you had been used to doing.

However, listening to the correct sound of English vocabulary is more useful than just using your hands in writing. In addition, speaking English vocabulary aloud on the basis of the correct English pronunciation which you can check out through the Internet or any other electronic devices has been proven to be better than only writing it down.

As you know, it is important to memorize English words and to repeat them continually. But learners must be patient in memorizing and repeating them. From the beginning until the end of the English learning process, you have to remember that you must be running on the right track in learning English.

Dajim Choi: Running on the right track? What does that mean?

Dr. Peter Lee: Let me give you a story in order to help you understand what it means.

You are actually "running" toward a goal every day. You are energetic and enthusiastic about "running" toward a goal because you have a dream. You are confident that you will reach that goal in the future as you are "running" without thinking about any irrelevant thing -- a good mindset that everyone should have. However, there is one question which is extremely important here. Do you think that the direction in which you have been running is right or wrong?

Dajim Choi: Direction? Do you mean the way that I am learning English, if it is right or wrong?

Dr. Peter Lee: That is what I am talking about. If you are striving to learn English in the wrong track, which indicates a wrong direction, your effort will be useless. Oh, I am sorry, "useless" may not be an appropriate word. Not useless but you may not get enough results even though you have made a lot of effort. If you memorize English vocabulary, which is the basic and fundamental block, it is going to be one of the elements of a huge and large English "castle" that you want to build with your knowledge. In order to prevent your English "castle" from stumbling or collapsing, you have to learn English the right way. Familiarizing yourself with English vocabulary is the first step to learning English and to building your English castle, preventing it from swaying and falling. This is exactly what I mean when I shared a story about "running on the right track."

Dajim Choi: Now I understand what you mean. I think I have to change the way I have previously used in memorizing English vocabulary since I started learning English. After listening to your lecture today, I realized what my faults were in learning English and why I could not speak English as well as others.

Dr. Peter Lee: Oh, wait a second! It is not your fault. It is really not your fault. You are doing well and you are a good student, as far as I know. The problem is the English educational system that we have had for more than fifty years. Until the 1980s there was no English listening examination in school. No one thought of its need because there was no English listening test in university entrance examinations. The English test for prospective students at universities was about comprehending English reading materials, English grammar, and English vocabulary. There was no examination pertinent to English listening.

Dajim Choi: But now, we are in different situation compared to the past. The English section of the university entrance examination now contains thirteen questions for listening out of fifty total. Do you think that this is the right direction for English education?

Dr. Peter Lee: Absolutely right! But I hope that more listening questions will be added.

Dajim Choi: Would you please tell me why?

Dr. Peter Lee: More listening questions should be added because listening is the first step to learning English as well as other foreign languages. Without listening practice, it would be impossible to learn English successfully, or other foreign languages. I am going to tell you more about this when I am introducing the right step to learning English. But now, we need to discuss the other methods written on the board.

## Discussion topic 5. Memorizing all the sentences written in English textbooks

Dr. Peter Lee: Someone recommended that memorizing all the sentences written in an English textbook is a good method to learn English. Who recommended this?

Pandan Gang: I did.

Dr. Peter Lee: Why don't you explain it in detail?

Pandan Gang: By all means! I have always thought of it as a shortcut to learning English. I mean, there may be an easier and quicker way to learn English. There are communicative competencies in English such as listening, speaking, reading, and writing. If I memorize all the sentences written in English textbooks, I don't need to worry about English grammar, English writing skills, and English vocabulary.

For example, memorizing an English word alone may be an erroneous way to learn English. While taking the subway or a bus, I used to memorize English vocabulary. But I could not use the words well because I was not sure whether the English sentences that I said were correct or not. I thought that one of the possible reasons was that I memorized only one English word contained in a sentence without looking at the full English sentence.

Then, I realized that memorizing a full sentence is a better way to learn English since it included new words. Memorizing entire English sentences in a textbook helped me not to worry about

English grammar. The infinitive, gerund, relative pronoun, and other grammatical structures were automatically and spontaneously understood by memorizing them all. In addition, I have chosen only English textbooks used in school because all the sentences written in the textbooks are correct. Many professors and professional writers worked together to make a textbook and to examine any mistaken expressions in it. The school's English textbooks could be a basic standard or guide in learning English.

Dr. Peter Lee: Your method seems to be such a good method. You don't want to spend any extra time examining whether English sentences are right or wrong. You also don't want to think about any complicated matters, such as English grammar. You hoped to discover the right way to learn English which reduces learning time. That is a shortcut. However, let me ask something about your method. Is it easy for you to memorize all of the sentences written in English textbooks?

Pandan Gang: Of course, it was not easy! I usually summarize ten sentences from English textbooks. It takes almost one hour to memorize them all.

Dr. Peter Lee: How many months did you do this process?

Pandan Gang: I think I did it for about six months.

Dr. Peter Lee: Do you intend to continue with this process in the future?

Pandan Gang: No. Actually, I gave up memorizing ten

sentences every day after six months for several reasons.

Dr. Peter Lee: What are these reasons?

Pandan Gang: I think that memorizing sentences is a burden. I had to memorize ten sentences every day. After a month, the number of sentences that I had memorized was almost three hundred. When the sentences began to accumulate, I started to forget the previous sentences I memorized. Then, I wondered how I will ever remember those sentences? Of course, I didn't want to forget all the sentences that I previously memorized because I spent too many hours mastering them all.

Dr. Peter Lee: Then, why did you recommend that method to us? From your experience, it doesn't seem like an enjoyable way to learn English.

Pandan Gang: But what is enjoyable in learning English? We have to study English really hard in order to use English really well. If I continually memorize English sentences, I believe that I can use English well someday. Do you know what is the real problem in my learning of English? The real problem is my attitude. I am not patient in learning English. I am not able to bear the hardship accompanying the learning of that language.

Dr. Peter Lee: Maybe or maybe not!

Pandan Gang: Why not? I know who I am. I am not good at English. My friends who know English better than me have more common sense. They are really patient. They don't easily give up on what they are doing. They keep memorizing English words and sentences every day. I don't know whether their English listening and speaking skills are better compared to mine because I have never seen or heard them speak with English native speakers. But they have good scores in English examinations at school.

Dr. Peter Lee: I don't want to know whether they are good English speakers and listeners or not. I want to focus on you and your problems, which prevent you from learning English.

There are two issues from your description. One is about whether English should be studied like other academic subjects. The other is about whether English learners should be patient or not. What do you think about the first issue? I hope that we can discuss freely any issue related to English education in Korea.

Pandan Gang: English should be regarded as another important academic subject. There is no doubt about this issue. We have been educated to learn English since the start of elementary school. English, indeed, is one of the major subjects that every student must learn.

Dr. Peter Lee: You are right. English is one of the major subjects handled in school. However, I think that you have not enjoyed the time you spent learning English. This can mean that in your school, learning and/or teaching English is approached too seriously.

English teachers require students to learn too much language structure. Some parts may be unnecessary, so those should be ignored in learning English. I don't know why students continue to learn unnecessary information related to English grammar, for example. Actually, when I was young, I studied English through an English grammar textbook, but it was too complicated and it involved many confusing parts which made me exhausted and distressed, physically and mentally.

Pandan Gang: Yes, you are right. I am very angry with English grammar textbooks. I don't want to be an English linguistic scholar. I just hope to listen to and speak English well. What I mean to say is that basic and general knowledge about English is needed in order to work with people who come from foreign countries. I have met many foreigners from Western countries and we had conversations in English. It was such a good experience for me because I could understand their Western cultural perspectives. Even though I could not correctly explain whatever I wanted to say in English, they all understood what I was saying. It was such a valuable moment in my life because it was my first time talking to foreigners in English.

Dr. Peter Lee: You don't need to be angry if you have difficulty with English grammar. I believe that sooner or later, you will find the right way of learning English. Even though you might make a lot of mistakes, don't worry about that. Mistakes are important so that you discover the right way to follow. I will tell you later my story about how many mistakes I made while learning English. Anyway, I am sorry to interrupt your story. So, how was it? How did you feel when you were talking to a foreigner in English for the first time?

Pandan Gang: It was an awesome feeling that I had never experienced before. Foreigners understood what I told them, although my facility in the English language was rather limited. I was actually excited about talking to foreigners in English so that I enjoyed studying English from that moment on.

Dr. Peter Lee: Did you also enjoy taking English classes in school?

Pandan Gang: No. In fact, taking English classes at school was kind of boring for me because there was too much information about English grammar that I had to memorize in order to get high scores on English examinations. That was why I started memorizing whole English sentences written in English textbooks: it was the simplest way that I know of to get high scores on English exams. I am not good at analyzing complicated grammar structures. I think that it would be easier for me to memorize English sentences without thinking about the underlying English grammar.

Dr. Peter Lee: Thank you for sharing your learning method and experiences obtained from the English educational system in Korea. I do agree with your positive feelings while talking to foreigners in English. I definitely have the same opinion as you about how boring English classes can be. But you have to always remember that English professors and educators are around to try to help you understand English. They are your helpers and mentors.

Pandan Gang: If the professors and educators are okay, then, what or where is the problem?

Dr. Peter Lee: The problem is not with English professors and educators but, actually, the English educational system of Korea. I believe that English education in Korea is going astray or has lost its focus. Let me ask you something. Why do you learn English? What is the main purpose of learning English?

Pandan Gang: My aim in learning English is to be able to speak English well. The main purpose in learning English is to get a good job after graduation. In addition, I believe that high scores on English examinations accredited by the government can be useful when I apply to companies. Submitting English scores on TOEFL (Test of English as a Foreign Language) or TOEIC (Test of English for International Communication) is mandatory when applying for jobs.

Dr. Peter Lee: Do you think that the way you are learning English at school now is the right path for you to improve your English listening and speaking skills?

Pandan Gang: Sadly, no! As you said, our English learning style is too serious and academic so that it is hard for us to understand English.

Dr. Peter Lee: Yes, that is what I am talking about!

If students are just learning English to prepare for English written and reading examinations, then their English language proficiency becomes very limited. Thus, I believe that the English education system of Korea should be changed so that English professors and educators also follow a new way to educate students in English. If English education administrators in Korea keep thinking only about reading and written examinations, I am sure that there will be no progress in English education.

Meanwhile, if they put too much emphasis on English grammar for exams, there is no improvement in English education. Therefore, if English education is too serious and academic for language learners, students may give up learning English because it becomes so tedious for them.

Pandan Gang: Can you give us an example of this?

Dr. Peter Lee: Of course! For example, when you look at explanations in English answer books, they seem to be useless for English learners because the discussion is too complicated and perplexing for English learners. Sometimes, the explanations in Korean of the English answers in books are quite long. It is hard for English learners to comprehend all of the Korean explanations about the English questions. In fact, some students may be confused no matter if they use an English or Korean textbook. Have you ever experienced this before?

Pandan Gang: Yes, I have. I have read a lot of detailed information from English reading materials, English grammar textbooks, English vocabulary textbooks, and others. However, I could not speak English fluently. How many hours and years have I been learning and studying English? My simple purpose is to listen to English and speak English well. It has been very hard for me. Thus, for several years, I have quit learning English. In addition, I am not a patient person for this specific type of learning.

Dr. Peter Lee: I see. Then, let me ask you something. What is your hobby?

Pandan Gang: You mean, anything related to English?

Dr. Peter Lee: No, I am just asking about your favorite hobby. Do you have any particular activity which you enjoy during your spare time?

Pandan Gang: Okay, I understand what you mean. Well, I really like dancing.

Dr. Peter Lee: You are a good dancer, aren't you? I am not good at dancing. I have danced in front of a mirror and looked at my dancing style. It was terrible! Even though nobody saw my reflection in the mirror except myself, I was embarrassed because of how I appeared. Then, I decided not to dance anymore, but to listen to dance music. That is enough for me. Anyway, why do you like dancing?

Pandan Gang: I like dancing because it is a kind of body language expressing my feelings. While I am listening to my favorite music, I just rely on my feelings and start dancing.

Dr. Peter Lee: Have you ever been tired of dancing? If yes, when did you feel tired? After one hour or two hours?

Pandan Gang: When you dance, there is no time limit for it. I just dance and enjoy how I feel while listening to favorite music. Even though I sweat a lot after one or two hours of dancing, I am happy and delighted with my moves.

Dr. Peter Lee: If you felt the same when you study English, would you make a decision to learn English?

Pandan Gang: I told you before, I am not good at English and I am not patient. After realizing the fact that English was so hard for me to understand, I gave it up for several years.

Dr. Peter Lee: I always think that learning English is quite similar to learning dance. I have never learned how to dance in dancing institutes but there is one similar characteristic between them. Both can be improved by regular practice. Let us imagine that you have been learning how to dance for several years and then you stopped dancing for a few years. Do you think that you could dance just like you did when you practiced regularly?

Pandan Gang: No, I have probably forgotten how to dance! My body has become too stiff, resulting in very graceless dance moves.

Dr. Peter Lee: That is right! You need to practice dancing regularly in order to stay in good shape for that activity. Now, this is very similar to learning English. You need to practice speaking and writing in English regularly to perfect the skill.

Learning English should be practiced without a pause. This includes training your tongue!

Pandan Gang: Did you say that we have to practice English using our tongue?

Dr. Peter Lee: Yes, definitely! You have to practice English using your tongue. Many students only focus on reading English materials, finding out the answers about the questions relative to English grammar, and memorizing English vocabulary. Are you using your tongue while learning English?

Pandan Gang: I usually use my eyes to read English materials and my brain to remember any grammatical knowledge that I studied in order to discover the right answers for English grammar examinations. When learning English vocabulary, I have not used my tongue, which means that I have almost never practiced reading English words aloud.

Dr. Peter Lee: If you close your mouth while learning English, how can you enjoy learning the English language?

When you are dancing, you are actually following a song and singing it because you move along to the beat that you are hearing. Your body is moving while your mouth is singing. After practicing a dance with music for a few minutes or hours, you may be satisfied with all the moves. Why don't you use that kind of sense when you are learning English?

Pandan Gang: I wish I could. But, how?

Dr. Peter Lee: Don't worry, I will teach you how.

First, open your mouth and use your tongue to speak English. Even though you don't know how to pronounce English words because you have never learned them before, you are just reading English aloud. Do you like pop music?

Pandan Gang: Yes, I do like pop music.

Dr. Peter Lee: Please tell me the title of a song that you like.

Pandan Gang: *Top of the World* sung by the Carpenters. Do you know this song?

Dr. Peter Lee: Yes, I really love that song! The song starts with the lyrics "Such a feeling coming over me…"

Pandan Gang: Yes. That is right!

Dr. Peter Lee: In my class, you are going to learn English by means of a pop song. Instead of learning English too seriously, I have to discover how to make you, especially those who have already given up learning that language because they find it boring and complicated, enjoy learning English. Would you please wait for my next class? I guarantee that you will never feel again that learning English is perplexing and even boring.

Pandan Gang: Okay. I will wait for the next classes and I hope that your teaching method will not be boring for us.

Dr. Peter Lee: That sounds like a warning.

Pandan Gang: No, I am just worried about how to start learning English again because, as I said, I have given up learning English several times. I am just worried about what I might turn out to be if I give up learning English once again.

Dr. Peter Lee: Alright. DON'T WORRY. Just take up the challenge again. If you give up on something, then, nobody else can help you start again. I implore you to change your mind!

We have had a long discussion of your learning method. This time around, why don't we discuss one of the other learning methods that other classmates wrote on the board.

## Discussion topic 6. Watching English dramas

Dr. Peter Lee: How about watching English dramas? Who recommended watching English dramas as one of the best ways to learn English?

Gamdong Min: I did!

Dr. Peter Lee: Would you please explain it in detail for us?

Gamdong Min: Yes. I really enjoy watching English dramas. Pandan Gang mentioned that learning English is not enjoyable and even unpleasant. However, I really recommend watching English dramas because, in my experience, it is really helpful for learning English.

Dr. Peter Lee: You are right. I will ask you one question. Do you understand all the dialogues in the English dramas that you watch? Our class is not for advanced level students, but for beginners or intermediate level students only. Your method can be useful only for advanced English students. Is that right?

Gamdong Min: No. I'm not at an advanced level yet. In addition, I cannot understand the entire sentences I hear in dramas. But watching their daily stories is fun and enjoyable. Do you know the drama *Friends*? I really enjoyed watching the series. Six major actors and actresses are in that drama. The drama is about how Americans live and describes events which might occur in their everyday lives. Thus, it is easy to understand Americans and what they are talking about to each other in their everyday lives. Their conversations are quite ordinary, natural, and funny. Many expressions that they say may be useful for English learners to learn and practice from. How about this method? What is your assessment?

Dr. Peter Lee: Your method is really good for English learners. Actually, watching English dramas is extremely useful for learning daily and natural expressions that Americans say. There are many kinds of drama and you can choose whatever you want. Some dramas are produced for kids and middle school or high school students. Other dramas are made for adults. In general, dramas are produced as a series, so audiences watch them sequentially.

There is another thing that English learners should remember. Watching an English drama may be helpful, but you should listen carefully to what actors and actresses are saying. But watching an English drama is definitely useful for English learners. There is no doubt about it. However, if you don't listen carefully to what they are saying, or you are just watching them without listening to them intently, you will not benefit from this experience.

Gamdong Min: What is the difference between watching a drama and listening to it?

Dr. Peter Lee: The biggest difference between the two activities is the use of the different parts of the body. When you are watching a drama, you are using your eyes to watch it and ears to listen to it. When you are listening to a drama without watching it, you are using only the ears to understand the message. That is the biggest difference.

Gamdong Min: I think everyone knows that already.

Dr. Peter Lee: Yes, I know everybody knows what I am saying! However, many people ignore the fact that they may lose their focus on listening to what actors and actresses are saying while watching a drama. It is called being distracted. The movements of actors and actresses in a drama and the background may be turning your attention away from what you are listening to. In order to help you understand what I am saying, I will give you an example.

There are two different situations involved.

For example, one person is watching a drama and the other person is listening to it with his eyes closed. The same scene repeats over and over. Who can better listen to the sound coming from the scene? Some may say that the watcher is a better listener because he can guess what actors and actresses are doing even if he cannot understand what they are saying. However, some may say that the listener is better than the watcher because he is focusing on listening alone. In addition, if he closes his eyes, he can focus more because he will not be distracted. It is hard to judge who is a better listener. But for those who continually listen, they become familiar with the sound of proper English and, therefore, later on, they become better English speakers. I am sure of this.

Gamdong Min: So, do you mean that I have to listen to a drama and not watch it?

Dr. Peter Lee: No, that is not what I am talking about!

I mean that you have to be careful when you are watching a drama. Do you know subtitles? When you are watching a foreign drama, you see translated sentences shown on the bottom of the screen. Those are called subtitles. Koreans who don't know English can understand English dramas through translated subtitles.

Gamdong Min: Actually, I didn't know the word subtitle at first. But based on your explanation, I understood what the word subtitle means.

Dr. Peter Lee: A subtitle can be a distraction when you are starting to improve your listening skills. Do you know why?

Gamdong Min: I don't know. I have usually thought that subtitles are useful for learning English. Without subtitles, I could not identify whether what I am thinking about the dialogue in a drama matches with what I actually heard. Reading subtitles can help me quickly understand the scene in a drama.

Dr. Peter Lee: Reading subtitles can be one trouble spot for you when enhancing your listening skills in English. Do you know how important listening is for learning English? Watching a drama can help you understand foreign cultures, different lifestyles and other aspects of life. However, if you want to enhance your listening skills in English, you should avoid looking at the subtitles in a drama. Instead, you should just listen to the words carefully.

Gamdong Min: What if I don't understand these words?

Dr. Peter Lee: Don't worry. You just need to watch it over and over without subtitles. In the case of your recommendation on watching an English drama, the bottom line of my instruction about your method is to watch and listen to it without any subtitles. You don't need to worry about whether you understand correctly what they are saying in a drama because you can comprehend their statements after watching it several times.

Gamdong Min: Is there a target percentage that I should aim to understand?

Dr. Peter Lee: If more than eighty percent of the statements spoken by the actors and actresses in a drama are familiar to you, then you should have no problem understanding what they are saying. This is very important.

You may not understand why eighty percent is proper and why you need to repeat it over and over until all the words spoken in a drama are familiar to your ears. I will explain it later. Actually, you need to know more precise information in order not to waste your invested time and effort for increasing your English ability by using dramas. Let us keep discussing this issue later.

Gamdong Min: Okay. I am looking forward to your precise recommendation later on about my suggestion.

## Discussion topic 7. Watching English news

Dr. Peter Lee: Let us now proceed to the other suggestions written down about the issue we are discussing – watching English news is next. Who suggested this? Would you please explain it more?

Mirae Kim: I did. News is the fastest and newest information that we can get through TV or the Internet. Watching the news cannot only be good for improving English listening skills but also for obtaining a lot of information. There are many things happening in our society. Politics, economics, and other social problems are handled and reported in the news so we can have various opportunities to broaden our horizons. In addition, news from all over the world is translated into English. For example: Arirang Radio News, CNN, BBC World, and many domestic and international news stations provide news in English. That is why I recommended watching news as definitely advantageous for improving our English ability.

Dr. Peter Lee: Great! You are absolutely right.

The news is a good source for learning English. There are many advantages when one listens to the news. News anchors are telling us the latest events using correct and accurate words which have been reviewed by news editors several times. Thus, there is no doubt that all the sentences that they are saying are correct. In addition, news anchors have correct and precise intonation and accents while speaking in English. Thus, that is also a great avenue for practicing speaking English.

Mirae Kim: To be honest with you, I have never thought about intonation and accents spoken by news anchors. However, their speech, including the correct intonation and accents, is an extremely good source for me to practice speaking English.

Dr. Peter Lee: You are right. However, there are advantages and disadvantages in using English news.

Mirae Kim: What are these?

Dr. Peter Lee: As you and I mentioned earlier, watching English news is beneficial to enhancing our listening skills. It also provides standard intonation and accents in speaking English. It is an important source of a lot of information which is related to domestic and international issues. However, we don't usually use the kind of statements spoken by news anchors in our daily lives. But ordinary conversations among news anchors in some shows can be a source of learning for all.

Mirae Kim: I can understand what you mean. There is no one who speaks in ordinary conversations like news anchors.

Dr. Peter Lee: Right. You and I are speaking, using many informal expressions. But news anchors are trained using formal sentences. Informal sentences and expressions such as *gotta, gonna, stuff*, and so on must be avoided in public news. In addition, the expressions that we generally use in daily communication are not formal. If there is someone who wants to improve his general speaking skill in English in the context of everyday life, then he needs to know useful expressions from dramas, movies, and so on.

Mirae Kim: Now, I understand what you mean.

Dr. Peter Lee: Watching news is certainly a good method to recognize the recent events happening in our society. It also helps that you improve your English composition skills. All the scripts that news anchors read during the news are a formal written document reviewed repeatedly. It would be hard to discover any wrong expressions or grammatical errors. Thus, watching news and reading the script spoken by news anchors can be useful, reliable, and trustworthy if you want to learn English.

I am just telling you that watching news is beneficial to enhance your speaking and writing skills as well as obtaining a lot of domestic and international information. I am not talking about whether all the news is useful, reliable, and trustworthy. Alright then, what is the next comment which helps people to learn English?

## Discussion topic 8: Using a telephone to converse with native speakers in English

Hana Moon: I am using a telephone program to converse with native speakers in English. It's very affordable.

Dr. Peter Lee: How does it work?

Hana Moon: I pick up the phone and dial. Then I am able to talk to native speakers in English. It also provides textbooks. On the phone, an English teacher and I talk to each other for ten to twenty minutes following the schedule that we made.

Dr. Peter Lee: That is a good source to practice listening to English and speaking English as well. Would you share any advantages to using a telephone program? And are there disadvantages in using a telephone program?

Hana Moon: One advantage is that the system is affordable; another advantage is that it can be used anytime at your convenience. If there is someone who cannot go to English institutes because of busy schedules, it is possible to learn English by phone. However, it may be hard to communicate using a telephone without seeing the person face to face.

For example, when you are talking to Korean people in Korean on the phone, you cannot see their gestures and other emotional expressions. That is why English learners have difficulty talking in English over the phone. Making conversation on the phone may be one of the hardest sessions for English learners. There are both advantages and disadvantages in taking an English program through the telephone. But I think that our discussion on the English program by phone is enough. Why don't we move to another topic?

## Discussion topic 9: Attending English language training programs in English countries

Dr. Peter Lee: The next recommendation for an English learning method is about attending English training programs in English countries. Who recommended this?

Soonsu Lee: I did.

Dr. Peter Lee: Would you please explain it in detail?

Soonsu Lee: I think that a learning environment can significantly influence a student who wants to learn English.

Dr. Peter Lee: Really? Your suggestion is very interesting to me. Why does a learning environment significantly influence students in learning English?

Soonsu Lee: It is obviously easy for us to meet Americans in the United States compared to meeting them in Korea. It means that there are many opportunities for us to practice our English in America because it is the native language. If I go to a grocery store, I probably have to use only English to communicate with workers in the store. That is a chance for me to practice my English. If I meet people on the street in order to ask directions, I also have to use English. If I am taking classes or any academic programs in America, there might be no way to converse with native speakers except in English. In general, Koreans think that going to America or any other English countries is helpful for them to learn English. That is why many Koreans are going to America, the United Kingdom, Australia, Canada, and New Zealand.

Dr. Peter Lee: It is definitely true that learning environments can affect students. In past decades, such a large number of people have gone abroad not only to learn English but also to achieve many other purposes such as getting into universities, getting jobs, or participating in academic conferences. But we are only focusing on English training programs in this discussion. In Korea, there are many English institutes where teachers from America and other English countries teach. Do you think that there may be significant differences between taking English training programs in English countries and taking them in Korea?

Soonsu Lee: I think that there are both similarities and differences. Taking English courses or programs in both English countries and Korea may be not too different because the teaching skills provided by native speakers may be quite similar. I have taken English programs in a private English institute in America and the skills were similar to those taught by native English teachers in private institutes in Korea. But the differences were that our classmates came from different countries such as China, Japan, Germany, and other African and European countries. I was very excited to meet and talk to them in English. We also had a picnic and prepared our respective traditional foods to share with others. It was such a great experience.

Dr. Peter Lee: You are right! That is such a great experience.

How long did you take English programs in America?

Soonsu Lee: It was almost nine months.

Dr. Peter Lee: Do you think that your English ability got better during the stay?

Soonsu Lee: I think so.

Dr. Peter Lee: I don't want to ruin your special and valuable experience obtained from English programs abroad. However, I would like you to evaluate whether your stay to learn English in America was successful or not. Would you please accurately evaluate your stay in America?

Soonsu Lee: Why?

Dr. Peter Lee: There are several reasons. Many students hope to study abroad and there is both something good and bad in this activity. If you give them some valuable advice, it may reduce any problems they might encounter. They may also be able to prepare more fruitful English training programs in those English countries.

Soonsu Lee: You are right. Actually, I thought that if I had prepared more before going to America, I could have progressed more with my English ability. No, I think MUCH MORE!

Dr. Peter Lee: Why?

Soonsu Lee: I just thought that taking English programs in America would be very helpful for me to enhance my English ability. It was just kind of a vague idea. It was just a hope.

Dr. Peter Lee: Yes, some students have the same or similar

expectation without any logical thinking that learning English in America will be much better. They think that staying in English-speaking countries will help them to learn English automatically. However, it is impossible for us to achieve something valuable without any effort.

Soonsu Lee: Yes, you are right. I just thought that I could have many chances to talk to people in English. In addition, their traditional cultures can help influence my English ability. However, it didn't go that way.

Dr. Peter Lee: Why? Do you think that English programs in America were not helpful and beneficial to you?

Soonsu Lee: No, it was a good program. In fact, I recommended it to my friends. Undergoing English training programs in English countries is advantageous. However, I just regret that if I had prepared my English ability before I attended the program, I would have succeeded in learning English more and gained much better English proficiency.

Dr. Peter Lee: What does the phrase *prepared my English ability* mean? Do you think that we have to prepare something before attending English programs in America?

Soonsu Lee: Yes, I do, if possible.

Dr. Peter Lee: What do we have to prepare? I think that we probably have some money to pay for tuition and fees. And we also have to rent a house and pay for breakfast, lunch, and dinner. Do you think that students who want to study abroad have to prepare those kinds of things?

Soonsu Lee: These things are very basic elements that students studying abroad need. But I am suggesting a different set of things.

Dr. Peter Lee: What are those?

Soonsu Lee: Students must study English hard before attending English training programs. Of course, if some students have enough money that their parents can financially support them and they could not care less about the money, then, I don't need to recommend this because this is related to money and effort.

Dr. Peter Lee: Related to money and effort?

Soonsu Lee: My father and mother work so hard to pay for our tuition and fees every year. I have one sister who is 19 years old. After becoming a university student, I kept telling my parents about learning English in America. However, they always turned down supporting me because of too much financial burden. I thought that if I studied English in America, I could give all my attention to learning English. In addition, one year might be enough for me to learn English and make people around me think that I was good at English. After one year of an English training program in America, I planned to continue developing my English capacity every remaining semesters before graduation.

Dr. Peter Lee: You are very good at planning your life. You

made a good plan even though you were just a freshman at university.

Soonsu Lee: Right. But actually many other university students plan their university life.

Dr. Peter Lee: Yes, you are right. But it would be hard to find somebody who sticks to her plan. Anyway, please keep explaining.

Soonsu Lee: I kept asking and persuading my parents that I had to go to America to learn English. They denied it for several months and I could not understand why they denied it, even though I already promised that I would study hard. I said that I was prepared! However, later on, I realized that it was such a big mistake.

My parents got bank loans and paid for my tuition and fees at last. I made a decision that I had to study hard in order to achieve my goal. I am sure this would make my parents very happy with all the results that I would get.

Dr. Peter Lee: So you did?

Soonsu Lee: I don't know. I could not say that I achieved everything that I intended before going to America. I think that I achieved fifty percent success and fifty percent failure.

Dr. Peter Lee: Why do you think that way?

Soonsu Lee: If I had prepared my English ability more when I was in Korea, I would have enhanced it in America much more. The United States is definitely a good place for me to learn

English and practice the language every day. There were tens of thousands of opportunities to talk to native speakers in English if I wanted to. However, the problem that I had was that I could not listen to English well. That was the biggest problem that I had when I was there in America.

Dr. Peter Lee: Why? You were not good at listening? You didn't develop your listening skills in English while here in Korea?

Soonsu Lee: Actually I didn't care about English listening skills. I just memorized English vocabulary and read many English sentences to understand them just like many students do when they are studying English in Korea.

Dr. Peter Lee: Oh my goodness! You were one of those Korean students who made a common mistake in learning English. Making a mistake means going to the wrong track when learning English. Was it hard for you to understand what Americans were saying?

Soonsu Lee: It was completely different compared to English that I had learned in Korea.

First, I ignored English pronunciation, intonation, and accents while learning English. In the case of English vocabulary, I just memorized those written in English textbooks. But there were so many unknown words that native speakers normally use in their life. I was especially astonished when I was watching advertisements on television which were spoken so fast. It was too fast for me to understand what it was all about. But later I understood that advertisements are delivered fast in order to provide a lot of information in a short period of time. Anyway, it was such a good experience which made me realize that I needed to train my English listening skills.

Dr. Peter Lee: You said that learning English in English programs in America is valuable, advantageous, and worthwhile. Now, I understand why you said those words: valuable and advantageous. There are good experiences which allow you to know what you need in learning English. These are also valuable opportunities to use English in America which can prove to be advantageous to you. But I don't get it about your experiences which may be worthwhile. Can you explain it in more detail, please?

Soonsu Lee: Thank you for asking that question. That is about the fifty percent failure that I mentioned earlier.

Dr. Peter Lee: Fifty percent failure?

Soonsu Lee: Yes, the word *worthwhile* is pertinent to time, money, and effort. The time, money, and effort that I spent could be much more worthwhile if I had prepared my English ability in Korea.

Dr. Peter Lee: Why? You wanted to learn English so you went to an English institute in America. You might have thought about how to use time, money and effort effectively and efficiently in order to learn English. Then, you finally persuaded your parents to go to the United States. Is it right?

Soonsu Lee: You are right. But I had to start from a class for beginners because I could not understand even simple questions that American teachers asked. They examined my listening, reading, and writing skills but, especially my listening skills needed a lot of improvement. Now, I am thinking… if I had listened to English well, I could have enhanced my English ability faster than I expected. My classmates from Europe and Africa could not read long English materials even if there were not many difficult words. I read them faster than other classmates. I asked them about how long you have studied English and they said that they had studied English for two years. In my case, I have studied English since elementary school and it has taken me more than ten years. However, they are good at speaking English compared to me. I didn't know why this happened to me. I started to listen to what they were saying in conversation and thought that they used many difficult expressions that I didn't know of.

Dr. Peter Lee: Really? Even though they had learned English for only about two years, but they used English better than you? I cannot believe this!

Soonsu Lee: It was also unbelievable for me, at first! I was very embarrassed that I could not speak English well even though I had studied English since elementary school. Then, I started thinking about what part is my fault for not speaking

English well. In order to find out the answer to the question, there was nothing that I could do with the exception of one thing, that is, to listen to what teachers and classmates were saying. I was wondering about how my classmates who learned English for only two years could speak English well and how it could be possible?

Dr. Peter Lee: Indeed, how was that possible? Please discuss it further.

Soonsu Lee: In the beginning, I just thought that since the languages have so much overlap in letters, it is easier for them. It might help them to speak English well even though the word order and sounds were different from each other. I have never conducted research about this issue and have never read any academic journals, thus, I don't know exactly how and why they were better English speakers than me. However, I found out one important thing from listening. They talked to each other using quite simple phrases and sentences. Their learning method was very simple. They just listened to each other and talked to each other. It seemed that they enjoyed learning English. Their learning method was completely different from how I had learned English. I have usually memorized English vocabulary and analyzed English grammar just like linguistic scholars who examined many specific structures and patterns of language. The starting point of my English learning method was absolutely different from what they did.

Dr. Peter Lee: Do you think that they were speaking English better than you because of only one reason, which is that they are just simply listening to and speaking English?

Soonsu Lee: According to my guess, that might be the answer which could explain the reason.

Dr. Peter Lee: I think that there is one more important reason. That is about also letters and listening. German and Spanish are composed of letters and they use their mother tongue which has the same alphabetic root. In addition, they are listening to and speaking their language which is composed of letters to which they are very accustomed. The grammatical order is also similar. Thus, they use English better than you even though they learned it for a much shorter period of time compared to you.

Actually, I don't want to say that the fundamental difference in English proficiency between Europeans and Koreans is the difference in their alphabets. There may be other reasons.

However, the way to overcome the difference is that Koreans must listen to English over and over in order to speak English well. That is the most important and fundamental cornerstone that Koreans must remember while learning English. I really like this sentence written in the Bible. "The stone you builders rejected, which has become the chief cornerstone (Acts 4:11)."

Soonsu Lee: Why do you like that verse from the Bible?

Dr. Peter Lee: The reason that I am using that sentence is because you have been studying English grammar, memorizing

English vocabulary, and reading English materials over and over without listening to English. However, you must change your mind from now on. You have rejected English listening practice which is the cornerstone of your English ability.

Soonsu Lee: Why is listening practice important?

Dr. Peter Lee: Oh, I am going to explain why English listening practice is important and how you have to practice it later. But, let me say that you had a very good discussion not only to know whether taking English training courses in English countries is good or bad but also to understand how to improve your English proficiency faster than your expectations. The answer is preparing your English ability before attending English programs in English countries. English ability is related to reading and writing skills and even English vocabulary. But the most important and basic language practice to enhance English ability is listening.

## Discussion topic 10: Participating in internship programs in English countries

Dr. Peter Lee: Alright then, let us discuss another topic. How about participating in internship programs in English countries? Who suggested this?

Seongsil Park: I did.

Dr. Peter Lee: Why don't you explain your suggestion in more detail?

Seongsil Park: I will do that now. I think that an internship program provides practical training opportunities to learn professional knowledge and skills. Students who are going to graduate from college or university shortly may use an internship program to better understand what they are doing and how they are doing it, if they get a job later on.

Dr. Peter Lee: What kind of job do you want to have after graduation?

Seongsil Park: I would really like to become a flight attendant on foreign airlines. Becoming a flight attendant not only on domestic airlines but also international airlines is my dream.

Dr. Peter Lee: Really? I see. Anyway, internship programs are a good chance to obtain theoretical knowledge as well as practical knowledge.

Seongsil Park: What is theoretical knowledge and practical knowledge?

Dr. Peter Lee: I don't want to talk about anything related to becoming a flight attendant because that is not the topic of our discussion. I want to talk about how to learn English.

In case of learning English, theoretical knowledge is about studying any academic knowledge related in English such as basic sentence structures, grammar, correct pronunciation, and many words and expressions that you learn from various English materials. Practical knowledge is about practicing English in a field such as internship programs. When you are meeting many customers during internship programs, you may feel that you need to study and practice English more. However, do you know the most important realization that you could gain during an internship program?

Seongsil Park: I don't know. What could it be?

Dr. Peter Lee: You may learn REAL English!

Seongsil Park: Real English? What is that?

Dr. Peter Lee: Yes, you may learn real English. Real English means that you are learning English which must be used in real and actual conversations. While talking to foreign customers, you have to use English. There is no way to avoid meeting foreigners in internship programs offered by international business companies. Especially in the airline industry, somebody who hopes to become a flight attendant in airlines or a ground worker for airports should have the English ability to make conversation with foreign customers.

Seongsil Park: Yes, you are right! That is why I participated in an internship program offered by an airline. I still remember the first day that I worked as an intern in the airline company. I thought that I could use English in front of foreign customers because I had learned and practiced English for a long time. However, it was totally a different feeling. In English textbooks, we learned formal dialogue and expressions which were repeated throughout the book. In the conversations with foreigners, I could not predict what they will say next. Thus, I could not think well and prepare for how I will respond.

In addition, some foreigners from non-English countries have uncommon English pronunciation so it was hard for me to understand their different pronunciations.

Dr. Peter Lee: Good! Yours was such a valuable experience that not many students might have. Your challenge is really good. How did you feel and what did you realize after completing the internship program?

Seongsil Park: The way I thought about learning English was totally changed.

Dr. Peter Lee: How?

Seongsil Park: I used to study English formally. But I just studied English in order to get high scores from accredited English examinations such as TOEFL, which is an abbreviation for Test of English as a Foreign Language. I don't mean that learning English in order to prepare for the taking of an English examination or to get higher scores is useless and meaningless. I mean that many students focus on getting higher scores from English examinations too much instead of having real English abilities. As you know, there are many students who have high scores on English examinations but there are not many students who can use effective English when talking to foreigners in English.

Dr. Peter Lee: You are definitely right. I have heard that some Korean applicants who apply for bachelor, master, or doctoral programs at colleges and universities in the United States have very high scores on the TOEFL examination. However, they are in trouble when they follow academic programs at university or graduate school in America. Some master or doctoral students are feeling this problem more seriously because they have to listen, speak, read, and write in English well. Usually, a few master or doctoral students in class discuss and argue controversial topics with each other in order to discover the best solutions. Professors suggest some important textbooks which may be helpful to discuss. Students have to read them all even if reading all the books that professors recommend is not mandatory. Actually, I didn't read them all but it is definitely true that reading more textbooks and getting more diverse information can be beneficial to win the discussion. That is why master and doctoral students spend more time reading various textbooks, newspapers, and journal articles. I am sorry that I changed the focus of the discussion. Anyway, it is true that

Korean students read English well and know English grammar but their weakness is the part of listening to English, speaking English, and writing down English sentences even though I don't want to always believe it.

Seongsil Park: Oh, really? I don't know about that because I have not been in master or doctoral programs in the United States. But I understand the point. The real English ability is doing well in listening, speaking, reading, and writing. The whole English communication competency is much more valuable than mastering only English examinations. Is that right?

Dr. Peter Lee: I agree. As you said, listening, speaking, reading, and writing English well is hard. It may take a long time to do that. Analogizing it further, it is important for you to eat various kinds of food, not to focus on only one food item. It means that many students are focusing on English examinations and getting high scores on them instead of obtaining useful English skills which can be used in real situations. Fortunately, nowadays, English listening skills are regarded with more importance in English examinations. This is the change which shows the better way of learning English. Thank you so much and it is a wonderful discussion that helps us to know what the real English ability is.

Seongsil Park: You are welcome.

## Discussion topic 11: Participating in working holiday programs in English countries

Dr. Peter Lee: Alright. What is the next discussion topic?

Gamsa Yang: The next topic about English learning methods is participating in working holiday programs in English countries.

Dr. Peter Lee: Did you recommend it?

Gamsa Yang: Yes, I did.

Dr. Peter Lee: Why don't you explain it in detail?

Gamsa Yang: In reality, this is not the best way to learn English but it could be useful if we find a good one which fits our individual purpose of learning English.

Dr. Peter Lee: That's interesting! Did you find an adequate and satisfactory position in working holiday programs according to your purpose?

Gamsa Yang: I don't know... Although it was fun, it was not of much help for me in developing my English ability. I participated in a working holiday program to learn not only English but also Western cultures. There are many kinds of working holiday programs and so I cannot explain them all. I couldn't guess if my experience of working holiday programs was a representative one.

Dr. Peter Lee: But I think that there may be something that you want to share.

Gamsa Yang: Yes, I have one thing to share. If students want to attend a working holiday program, they have to think about precisely what they want. Many students think that they can learn English as well as earn money which can be spent on accommodation, transportation, and other various expenses while working in English countries.

Dr. Peter Lee: Yes, many students have the same opinion before participating in working holiday programs.

Gamsa Yang: I participated in a working holiday program not only to learn English but to experience different cultures. I was wondering about how different people from different countries think. In addition, I was eager to learn something new and meet someone far from home.

Dr. Peter Lee: So did you meet many new people and learn about different cultures from a working holiday program?

Gamsa Yang: Actually I didn't meet many people but I learned something new from various activities. Now, I can talk to foreigners in English without difficulty even though I am not really good at English. I lived with English-speaking families and talked to them in English. At first, they could not understand what I said. But after several months they started understanding my English.

Dr. Peter Lee: It seems that it worked well for you because it was not difficult for you to talk to English native speakers.

Gamsa Yang: Yes, but I am afraid that you and my classmates might think that I am very good at English already. I talk with foreigners using simple English words only, meaning without difficult and professional expressions. As you know, I was not in undergraduate, master, or doctoral programs but in a working holiday program. People working with me talked to me using simple words because we worked together in the field not in class. If there is someone who wants to learn English which is used in everyday life, a working holiday program is good. It also helps you to gain various cultural experiences. However, if you want to get professional knowledge and enhance your English ability more intensively, the working holiday program is not a good fit for you.

Dr. Peter Lee: I definitely have the same opinion as you. Basically, working holiday programs are extremely different from academic programs. Students should evaluate their purpose in attending a working holiday program and figure out what kind of benefits it offers. I think that, now, you are not worried about how to speak and what to say when you meet foreigners, right? That may be the benefit that you have gained from attending the working holiday program.

Gamsa Yang: Yes, you are right! I am not worried about meeting foreigners because their thoughts are similar to my thoughts. Of course, there are some big differences between our ways of thinking and theirs. But we are nothing more than human beings. It means that we are, basically, equal.

Dr. Peter Lee: Oh, good! You really broadened your horizons from the working holiday program. Great!

Gamsa Yang: Right. But I am studying English hard because my expressions in English are limited. In addition, I would like to attend academic programs in order to improve my professional English ability. One working holiday program experience was enough for me to form close relationships with English native speakers. Now, it's time for me to enhance my professional and academic knowledge in English from English programs at school.

Dr. Peter Lee: Good! Thank you for sharing your experience gained from working holiday programs in English countries. The point of your story is that there are many advantages to participating in a working holiday program. However, these programs may not be appropriate for English learners who hope to obtain professional and academic knowledge in English.

Gamsa Yang: Yes, that is my point.

## Discussion topic 12: Taking private lessons from native English speakers

Dr. Peter Lee: Then, let us discuss another topic. What about taking private lessons from native English speakers? Who suggested this method for learning English?

Mi Jang: I did. I think that taking a private lesson is effective and efficient for learners. Compared to other subjects, English is a subject which is not effective and efficient to learn when too many students are learning at the same time in the same class. In general, students have different English levels. That is why schools should offer different levels of English classes separated into beginners, intermediates, and advanced students. However, many schools still provide English classes in which all the different levels of students study in the same class. It is not helpful for them to learn English effectively and efficiently.

Dr. Peter Lee: I think so. What kind of private lessons have you taken?

Mi Jang: I was not good at English when I was a middle school student and I could not follow lectures provided by English teachers. That was why I had to start taking private English lessons. A private tutor taught me English both in Korean and English. He explained English grammar so I could understand basic grammar. He also helped me to read English textbooks and interpret them in Korean.

Dr. Peter Lee: But you recommended for us to take private

lessons taught by English native speakers.

Mi Jang: Yes, I did. I would just like to compare the effectiveness of learning English between Korean tutors and English tutors.

Dr. Peter Lee: Is there a significant difference in learning English between the two of them?

Mi Jang: There are good points and bad points to both of them.

Learning English from Korean teachers was good for helping me to understand basic English, but my Korean teacher, who was about twenty-two years old, was not good at speaking English. He explained English grammar and interpreted English sentences so that it was easy for me to understand basic English. In addition, the private lessons were not expensive. However, he didn't teach me how to listen to English and what I had to practice in order to improve my listening skills. I guess the reason is that he himself didn't practice his listening skills. His lectures were powerful for helping me to read English sentences and understand English grammar. That was helpful for me to get good scores on English examinations at school because English examinations at school were about English grammar and reading.

Dr. Peter Lee: What about tutoring from English native speakers?

Mi Jang: I had a private teacher who was an English woman, and she could not speak Korean at all. She explained every bit of grammar in English. Actually she was not good at English grammar.

Dr. Peter Lee: Really? She didn't know English grammar but taught English, right?

Mi Jang: No, she didn't, but I can understand her now.

Dr. Peter Lee: Why?

Mi Jang: I think that she didn't know English grammar because her major at college was not English education. Similarly, I could teach Korean even though I don't know Korean grammar well.

Dr. Peter Lee: Now I understand what you mean. I think that your listening and speaking skills were very quickly advanced by her lecture.

Mi Jang: Yes, indeed. She talked to me only in English and I had to understand what she said. It was hard for me to understand her teaching because I was not accustomed to the pronunciation spoken by an English native speaker. I think that taking lessons from English native tutors is one of the best ways to develop listening and speaking skills in English.

Dr. Peter Lee: I think that it is difficult to afford private lessons, isn't it? How much money did you pay for that?

Mi Jang: I paid 50 dollars per hour. I took four hours per week, and sixteen hours per month in total. The total payment was about 800 dollars.

Dr. Peter Lee: Really? 800 dollars per month! It was really

expensive! If I were your father, I would not have paid that much!

Mi Jang: After two months, I quit taking private lessons because it was too expensive. If I had a million dollars, I would have taken that kind of private lesson without caring about the money.

Dr. Peter Lee: Oh, be careful. There are many ways to learn English and some methods might be much better than the private lessons taught by native English speakers. I think that your recommendation could be helpful and useful for some people who have a lot of money. That method would not be useful for everyone.

Mi Jang: I think so, too.

Dr. Peter Lee: Many people misunderstand that taking private lessons is good for helping them to learn English quickly. Perhaps, others think that taking private lessons is better than taking group or public lessons for learning English. However, this may be right and this may be wrong, depending on their purpose and the intrinsic nature of the learner. What is the most important thing that you have to consider when you learn English?

Mi Jang: I don't know about that. If I knew precisely how to learn English, then I would not need to take private English lessons. However, I still don't know how to learn English, even after taking expensive private lessons from English native speakers. What should I do?

Dr. Peter Lee: Don't worry. This is the way for us to figure out what is the right manner to learn English. First, you have to examine what you have done in order to assess the good points and bad points of your experience. If your method of learning English is inefficient, you have to discover why you didn't get successful outcomes in learning English. We are going to find an efficient way to learn English in the second part of this session.

## Discussion topic 13: Reading English textbooks and newspapers

Dr. Peter Lee: But for now, let us discuss another topic. What about reading English textbooks and newspapers? Who suggested this?

Danbi Son: I did.

Dr. Peter Lee: Would you please explain it more?

Danbi Son: Yes, I will. I have been thinking that reading English textbooks and newspapers is one of the best ways to learn English. My parents always said that reading is definitely an important part of learning a language. They said that someone who reads a lot of textbooks can speak well. When reading textbooks more and more, we are gradually attaining a lot of valuable information. A lot of valuable information may be transferred into professional knowledge. Someone who is continually getting information after reading many textbooks can get smarter than before. Does that make sense?

Dr. Peter Lee: Yes, it makes sense! But you continually mentioned textbooks. What are some factors to consider in choosing a textbook for learning English?

Danbi Son: I think that textbooks are written, edited, and revised by professors, researchers, practitioners, and others who have professional information and knowledge. People think of them as experts. They have been professionally trained for a long time. Their knowledge and wisdom is translated into written words. Those written words and sentences are published in a textbook so that the quality of most textbooks is really high.

Dr. Peter Lee: You are right. If the quality of a textbook is high, then, students can trust all the information written in it.

Danbi Son: Yes, that is why I have chosen English textbooks.

Dr. Peter Lee: But are there any weaknesses in English textbooks?

Danbi Son: I don't know about that.

Dr. Peter Lee: English textbooks are written for all students who are learning English. Students are obtaining general information from English textbooks. General information means it is generic for everyone – texts that are not too hard to understand because they are made for every reader to understand. The information written in English textbooks is not too hard, is it? In the case of English textbooks used in middle and high school, their levels are not too high either.

Danbi Son: That's right. My friends usually have three or more English reference books for learning English other than their English textbooks. They have used other English reference books for learning English grammar, speaking, reading, and writing. They need many English reference books related to their English textbook because the content of their textbook may not be enough. When we are taking an English examination, which may be complicated, we definitely need additional English reference books. This is because additional reference books can have more useful information.

Dr. Peter Lee: But you recommended for your classmates to read English textbooks.

Danbi Son: Yes, I did. That is also right because English textbooks are fundamental for beginners who are learning English. The content of English textbooks provides information which is basic, so English learners should at least know it.

Dr. Peter Lee: Now I understand why you recommend English textbooks. However, you have to avoid underestimating the content of English textbooks. Some students misunderstand or underestimate the quality of English textbooks. They think that reading additional English reference books for English grammar, reading, vocabulary, and others is more important than reading only English textbooks. That is not true at all! Let's play a game using numbers in order to help you understand what I mean to say. Two times two equals?

Danbi Son: Four.

Dr. Peter Lee: Nine times seven equals?

Danbi Son: Sixty three.

Dr. Peter Lee: What about twenty two times five equals?

Danbi Son: One hundred ten. But why are you asking me this numbers question? This is not math class.

Dr. Peter Lee: I know! But I am trying to help you understand the basics of English by calculating numbers. You learned how to calculate numbers when you started math class. When you started math, you probably understood how to add, subtract, multiply, and divide by using simple numbers. Now you can calculate difficult numbers on the basis of the knowledge that you learned when you were young. The same phenomenon can be applied to learning English.

Danbi Son: Could you tell us how?

Dr. Peter Lee: I'd be glad to. You learned the basics from English textbooks at school. Even though the knowledge that you obtained from your English textbooks is easy, you can use it in any situation. Simple English sentences in English textbooks can be combined in order to create new sentences. It is called the multiplier effect. You can make many sentences using the basic sentences that you learned from English textbooks. In any kind of academic subject, the basics are important in order to understand any profound, complicated and philosophical knowledge. Can you understand the reason I am insisting on basic knowledge obtained from English textbooks?

Danbi Son: Yes, I can, now.

Dr. Peter Lee: Very good. You are smart and learn quickly.

Danbi Son: Thank you so much!

Dr. Peter Lee: What about reading English newspapers? Is it a good method to learn English? If yes, can you explain it more?

Danbi Son: Of course. I have heard that newspapers are a great resource for learning English. In Korean classes, teachers told me that reading Korean newspapers would be very helpful for enhancing reading skills and obtaining professional knowledge.

Dr. Peter Lee: You are right. A newspaper is a publication which provides a lot of information including news, opinions, and any other valuable facts. The many advertisements also allow readers to get necessary information that they need. In the case of opinion columns, that is useful for learning how to write English sentences correctly. Usually one column is comprised of 1,500 to 2,000 words. Columnists indicate their opinions about problems and share possible solutions. The columns are one of the best resources for English learners. One more thing which is important is that newspapers are written in contemporary English so that the vocabulary written in a newspaper is definitely useful. In addition, all the expressions and phrases written in a newspaper are formal English writing so that the newspaper is the best example for learning official, professional, or business English. Last but not least, reading English newspapers is very interesting to me. I am able to learn what happened in the past, what is happening at the present, and what will happen in the future through newspapers. A newspaper is a kind of resource for understanding the past and present and for predicting the future.

Danbi Son: Yes, that is right! I am also interested in reading newspapers. Especially exciting are word games in newspapers, which are called crosswords. I need to know English vocabulary and practice it daily. Crosswords are good word games for me to guess the matching word for many questions. They help me to remember the words that I have learned. Do you know how extremely happy I am after figuring out all the answers to a crossword?

Dr. Peter Lee: Yes, I can guess how you feel a little because I used to do the same thing when I read newspapers. Thank you for sharing your method of learning English. Please keep doing it and it will help increase the power of your English vocabulary.

## Discussion topic 14. Making friends who come from English-speaking countries

Dr. Peter Lee: Now, let us talk about another topic. Someone wrote on the board that making foreign friends who came from English-speaking countries is good for learning English. Who recommended this?

Nara Lee: I did.

Dr. Peter Lee: Oh, you are the class representative. I think that you have many friends here because becoming a class representative means that many students like you. Basically, we are all friends, but you are the leader of the students in this class. So I guess that you are suggesting this method because it is related to forming a relationship with people. Is that right?

Nara Lee: Yes, that is right! Actually, I like people. Talking and sharing information and opinions is good for helping me to understand what other people are thinking and doing. It is a truly beneficial method for broadening my horizons. I also wonder about what foreigners are thinking and doing. I assume that their culture and lifestyles are different from mine, so that their ways of thinking are most likely dissimilar from mine as well.

Dr. Peter Lee: Have you ever experienced that?

Nara Lee: Yes, I have. On Sunday I go to church and meet many foreigners. The church where I go is popular among foreigners who are visiting Korea for a while, or staying in Korea for a few years. After attending Morning Service, there is

Bible Study with group members. The group members are Koreans, Korean-Americans, Americans, Canadians, and others from diverse ethnic backgrounds. It is a very good opportunity to share not only Christianity, but also various opinions.

Dr. Peter Lee: What realizations have you had out of this experience?

Nara Lee: After talking to each other, I realized that racial and cultural differences are not barriers to understanding each other. Actually, I was very afraid in revealing my opinion because I was worried about what other group members would think about it. When I attended the first meeting, I thought there might be a gap between our thoughts, since we come from different cultural backgrounds.

Dr. Peter Lee: Do you think that you are different from them?

Nara Lee: I definitely think that we are all different, but we have one thing in common: the intent for all to understand and respect each other.

Dr. Peter Lee: That is what you call mutuality in thought and mind.

Nara Lee: Right. I hesitated to share my opinion, but other group members also hesitated to share theirs. One of the group members from America said that she had many friends and stuck their pictures on a mirror to look at them and remember them every day. However, she felt alone because they haven't met each other for a long while, so their relationships were slowly disappearing. But I said that we can be new friends, and what I said delighted her!

Dr. Peter Lee: Good! You are a really good person. Your group members, who are called a minority, need some help. When you share your opinion and listen to their opinions, they can feel happy.

Nara Lee: I am also happy not only to gain new friends from Bible Study at church, but also to converse with them in English. Every Sunday I meet and talk with them in English, so that I can practice the language and make more ethnic friends.

Some friends in that group want to learn Korean because they are Koreans but they cannot speak Korean well. I can understand them one hundred percent because they were born and raised in America so it is hard for them to use Korean.

Anyway, there are many benefits if we speak English well.

Making a lot of friendships with foreigners is one of the best benefits for someone who can speak English well. English is not my mother tongue; that is why I have some difficulty in talking with foreigners in English. However, attending Bible Study with foreigners every Sunday at church has motivated me to keep learning and practicing English.

Dr. Peter Lee: But I think that might be hard for you to continually attend Bible Study. They are better speakers than you in English because they are native speakers whose mother tongue is English.

Nara Lee: Yes, you are right. It was hard at the beginning and uncomfortable even up to now.

Dr. Peter Lee: Why?

Nara Lee: Because I have to use only English and, sometimes, there is a limit to what I can explain well and the things I want to express.

Dr. Peter Lee: If you still feel uncomfortable, why are you still attending Bible Study?

Nara Lee: If I judge what I have gained and lost, I would like to think that I have gained much more than what I have lost.

Dr. Peter Lee: What is something that you have gained and what is something that you have lost?

Nara Lee: I have gained many foreign friends and developed my English ability. If I hadn't taken up the challenge to attend this Bible Study, I wouldn't have made a lot of friendships with foreigners and couldn't have developed my English ability. No one pushed me to attend and it was purely my choice and determination. I feel that it was such a good decision. In addition, I have gained diverse perspectives for understanding people who were born and raised in different countries. My ability to understand has improved a lot compared to before. As a result, my dream has totally become attainable since I met my foreign friends.

Dr. Peter Lee: What is your dream?

Nara Lee: My dream is to work for international organizations such as the World Tourism Organizations or the WTO. I like to travel and meet people. The WTO is the perfect organization for me to travel all over the world and to meet people from all walks of life.

Dr. Peter Lee: Awesome! Then, what is something that you have lost?

Nara Lee: I wanted to become an official who works for the government because a public position is stable and many students prefer it. As you know, our society is rapidly changing and more people hope to possess stable and secure occupations. But I abandoned that idea after making foreign friends. My foreign friends travel a lot and meet so many people around the world. I thought that I had just been aiming to become someone who will be reputable, excellent, and honorable. I mean that I cared about what other people around me thought about me. However, my foreign friends care about what they really want to do for their own happiness. They have different mindsets which seem more free, dynamic, and energetic, without thinking about what other people are concerned about. I think that they are enjoying their lives more because they are able to pursue their dreams. They are more focused compared to me.

Dr. Peter Lee: You can make your life enjoyable as well. But you have to find a balance between studying hard to pursue your dream and having fun in your life at the same time.

Nara Lee: Actually, I didn't lose anything. I have set my mind to look at the world in a different way. It is hard to achieve two goals at the same time. One goal is to achieve my dream and the other is to make my life energetic and exciting which, in my opinion, is the way to happiness.

Dr. Peter Lee: Let me ask something. Did you give up becoming an official of the World Tourism Organization?

Nara Lee: No, I didn't give it up. I still have that dream but I want to be involved in many activities in order to obtain diverse experiences and perspectives. One thing that I lost is the mindset that I had before, that is, focused on only becoming a reputable and well-known person in the world by studying hard without caring about other factors that can entertain my life. As a result, my life was not exciting and fun at all. However, my foreign friends helped me change my mind. During the conversation with them, they shared their diverse and exciting experiences, adventures, and activities that I also wanted to do.

Dr. Peter Lee: But I am worried that you are not focusing on studying as a student.

Nara Lee: No, they do focus on their studies and dreams at the same time. They are using their time effectively and efficiently. They seem like adults and think about their responsibilities as well.

Dr. Peter Lee: So, they are trying to find a balance between what they have to do in order to pursue their dream as a student and what can entertain them or what makes them happy. They realize that time is never turning back for them.

Nara Lee: That's what I am talking about. I am also studying hard to achieve my dream, which is becoming an official at the World Tourism Organization, and traveling a lot to meet people around the world on vacation. Thus, time must be used carefully.

Dr. Peter Lee: It is called time management.

Nara Lee: Yes, I am trying to use time, which is limited, more efficiently and productively.

Dr. Peter Lee: Your experience makes me very happy and enthusiastic. You are also very confident about what you are doing to achieve your dream.

Nara Lee: Yes, that is one of the important things that I have gained from my conversations with foreign friends. I am really happy to talk to foreigners in English because it widens my horizons. I love Korea, where I am living, but I also would like to live abroad and meet diverse people. My work field is not going to be only in Korea, but in the world. I want to work with foreigners and try to expand the range of my business activities to the world.

Dr. Peter Lee: Oh, great! It is such an amazing and wonderful dream and I definitely believe that you will achieve your dream. I really would like to say one thing. To dream is to make your life more fruitful and hopeful. You have to say positive words instead of negative words. You have to believe that you can achieve your dream. Do you know why? The words that you say have power. I really love this sentence written in the Bible. "The tongue has the power of life and death, and those who love it will eat its fruit (Proverbs 18:21)."

Nara Lee: That is a good sentence! I'd love to memorize it. In the past, I just learned English because I had to take English examinations and have good scores on them. My only focus in learning English was having good scores on English examinations. There was no more reason because I had not thought about broadening my horizons by learning English. If I had only focused on English examinations, I would not have been concerned about using English in real situations, just like forming a lot of relationships with foreigners. I also would not have changed my dream to my real dream! Now I am eager to motivate myself by learning English. I really hope to use English more fluently and understand what English native speakers are saying perfectly. When I read an English book now, the way I read it has become totally different. When I considered only English examinations, I studied English grammar and memorized a lot of English vocabulary in order to get higher scores on English examinations than other classmates. But now, I am considering how to use English vocabulary, how to talk to foreigners in English, and how to write down English sentences. It is a real English learning process. It is definitely much more fun and exciting.

Dr. Peter Lee: You are so great! You have totally opposite

perspectives compared with many students who still focus too much on English grammar, which is not very useful.

Nara Lee: Thank you for your encouragement and compliment! Actually you are right. No Americans care about whether their statement is grammatically correct or not. There is no Korean who thinks about Korean grammar first while talking with someone in Korean.

Dr. Peter Lee: I think that you lost nothing but gained many things. After you started to talk to foreigners in English, you realized that the method by which you learned English was totally wrong, so you changed your mind about learning English. Your practical knowledge gained through a practical learning method by meeting foreign friends led you to the right path to learning English. Many students who study in America, Canada, or other English-speaking countries realize that they have to study English again from the BEGINNING. Do you know what the reason is?

Nara Lee: No, I don't. Please tell us.

Dr. Peter Lee: Yes, I will. They cannot understand what English native speakers say, even simple words! They have learned English since elementary school, making it more than ten years. Even though they have studied English for more than ten years, and have spent so much money, they cannot listen to and speak English well. What is the problem? The most serious problem is that they only considered English examinations, which are organized to test only reading and English grammar. Many people would say that those tests are disappearing as time goes by. However, that is not true. There are lots more students who can read English well and know about English grammar than students who can listen to English well and speak English well. What is the more important competency among listening, speaking, reading, and writing in English usage? What do you think is the first thing that you have to know and practice? The answer is going to be taught in the second session of my lecture.

## Discussion topic 15: Reading English materials aloud every day

Dr. Peter Lee: Okay, let us talk about another topic in learning English. Someone suggested that reading English materials aloud every day is a good method of learning English. Let us discuss this. Who recommended this?

Damdae Han: I did.

Dr. Peter Lee: Why do you read English materials aloud?

Damdae Han: Because I want to speak English well.

Dr. Peter Lee: Do you think that reading English materials aloud is helpful for you to speak English well?

Damdae Han: Yes, I do.

Dr. Peter Lee: Really? Do you think so?

Damdae Han: Of course.

Dr. Peter Lee: Alright. Why don't you read the following sentence? *"I should've done it."*

Damdae Han: *I should'be done it.*

Dr. Peter Lee: No, no. *I should've done it.*

Damdae Han: *I should'be done it.*

Dr. Peter Lee: No, no. Your sound is different from mine. Do you notice some differences between your pronunciation and my pronunciation?

Damdae Han: No, your sound and my sound are almost the same and it is hard to find out significant differences.

Dr. Peter Lee: Really? You have to listen to the sound carefully spoken by me. Let's listen again and follow the sound. *"I should've done it."*

Damdae Han: *I should'be done it.*

Dr. Peter Lee: No, no. *I should've done it.*

Damdae Han: *I should'be done it.*

Dr. Peter Lee: Why don't you close your eyes and listen to it carefully. *"I should've done it."*

Damdae Han: *I should'be done it.*

Dr. Peter Lee: Let's try another one. *"I have faith."*

Damdae Han: *I habe pace.*

Dr. Peter Lee: No, that is not right. *"I have faith."*

Damdae Han: *I habe pace.*

Dr. Peter Lee: No, you can diagnose the problems of your pronunciation by careful listening. Your pronunciation problems must be diagnosed and corrected.

Damdae Han: Do you think that my pronunciation is wrong?

Dr. Peter Lee: Yes, your pronunciation is wrong.

Damdae Han: I have never thought about whether my pronunciation is right or wrong.

Dr. Peter Lee: That is the biggest mistake that many students who are learning English make commonly.

Damdae Han: I just memorize and read English sentences aloud. That is a good way to improve my speaking skills.

Dr. Peter Lee: I am really sad when many students overlook common mistakes in incorrect English pronunciation.

Damdae Han: What is the mistake that many students commonly make?

Dr. Peter Lee: They don't check correct pronunciation before reading English sentences aloud. Do you think that English pronunciation is the same as Korean pronunciation?

Damdae Han: No.

Dr. Peter Lee: Then, why didn't you check and examine any different pronunciations?

Damdae Han: I didn't need to examine them because there was no need to pay attention to them. There is no question or test at school about English pronunciation.

Dr. Peter Lee: Basically, your method is right to enhance your speaking skills, except one thing. That is about checking the correct pronunciation before you practice reading English sentences aloud.

Damdae Han: Oh, really? I have never thought about the correct English pronunciation while learning English.

Dr. Peter Lee: I feel sorry about that. But you should always check the correct pronunciation if you want to learn English correctly.

Damdae Han: Why?

Dr. Peter Lee: English is totally different from Korean. As you know, the shape and sound of the letters is different. But the biggest differences between Korean and English are sound, intonation, and accent. English has F, TH, V, L, and other sounds, but there are no such sounds in Korean. When you were reading the sentence *"I should've done it"*, you read it aloud like *"I should'be done it."* You didn't know the difference between the B and V sounds. Even though you have seen the word HAVE millions of times, you could not identify what the word was. I read another sentence aloud which is *"I have faith."* But you repeated it just like *"I habe pace."* You don't know the V sound, F sound, and TH sound. Probably, Koreans can understand what you are saying even though your pronunciation is wrong because Koreans are familiar with the English words spoken with Korean pronunciation. However, Americans and other English-speaking people cannot understand what Koreans are saying in English because they are not familiar with English spoken by Koreans.

Damdae Han: Oh my God! I have practiced reading English sentences without checking the correct English pronunciation. I have done it for about a year and a half.

Dr. Peter Lee: Don't worry about that. You are fine. Do you know that there are more people who practice reading English sentences aloud without ever checking the correct pronunciation?

Damdae Han: Oh my goodness! Their efforts may be in vain. They should know how important pronunciation is in learning English.

Dr. Peter Lee: You know that the correct pronunciation is important not only in English but also in any language. A language is composed of a set of sounds and written letters. A set of sounds is important to listening and speaking. And written letters are also significant for you to read and write. In terms of speaking skills, you must consider both listening and speaking. Do you know why?

Damdae Han: I don't know.

Dr. Peter Lee: If you listen to the sounds correctly, you can pronounce it correctly as well.

Damdae Han: Really?

Dr. Peter Lee: There may be some variations from person to person. However, it is hard to find a case when someone who listens to the correct pronunciation well has the wrong pronunciation. For example, I heard that a person who is blind was hired by a radio station. Even though she is blind, she spoke English very well using the correct pronunciation. The radio station needed a person who announces news using precise pronunciation for every listener. Do you know why she listens to the sound better than others? This is because she can focus more on listening to the sound than others because she is not distracted by anything.

Damdae Han: What about the case of a deaf English learner?

Dr. Peter Lee: The deaf need captions written underneath the picture on television, which shows the words spoken by people. If they have never listened to the sound, they cannot know what the right sound is. Thus, they cannot make the right sound because they have never listened to it. Does that make sense?

Damdae Han: It makes sense.

Dr. Peter Lee: The bottom line in the case of your suggestion is that you have to check the correct pronunciation before you practice reading English sentences aloud so as to avoid wasting all your effort. Do you know what I mean?

Damdae Han: Yes, I do. Thank you so much for telling me this valuable information. Now, I know how to practice reading.

## Discussion topic 16: Listening to and singing English songs

Dr. Peter Lee: Let us discuss another topic. What about listening to and singing English songs?

Bada Song: I'd love to listen to and sing English songs.

Dr. Peter Lee: Oh, great! Why do you think that listening to and singing English songs are good methods of learning English?

Bada Song: That is the most efficient method of learning English from my point of view.

Dr. Peter Lee: Why?

Bada Song: There is synergy between what I want to do and what I have to do. I want to increase my English listening skills by listening to my favorite English songs. My theory is that students who are doing what they want to do can focus more on it, even if it is difficult.

Dr. Peter Lee: You are right! Do you like English?

Bada Song: Actually I didn't like English. But I had to study English in preparation for English examinations at school. Thus, I needed to find a way to learn English. I had to make myself familiar with English.

Dr. Peter Lee: So you chose English songs, right?

Bada Song: Yes, that's right. I usually listen to Korean songs and follow them. I didn't know the lyrics of songs that I heard at first. But after repeating them over and over, suddenly, I was able to follow them. Even though I could not correctly sing the lyrics of a song at the beginning, the sound and the lyrics had become familiar to me as I listened to it repeatedly. As a result, I just believed that listening to English songs would be a good method for learning English.

Dr. Peter Lee: Now I understand what you mean and why you are using English songs in order to learn English. Can you think of other benefits that you could obtain while using English songs as an English learning instrument?

Bada Song: No, I cannot think of other benefits.

Dr. Peter Lee: What about the difference between the Korean and English languages?

Bada Song: You have already mentioned that English is comprised of rhymes, intonations, and accents which the Korean language does not have.

Dr. Peter Lee: Yes, you are right. That is the answer. Using English songs can be useful for you to learn not only English expressions but also intonation and accent. The intonation of English is related to the sound which is rising and falling. The accent of English is pertinent to specific tones expressed. Nobody speaks Korean like he or she is singing a song. However, speaking English is a bit similar to the sound of a song.

Bada Song: Now I understand that using English songs has a lot of benefits for learning English.

Dr. Peter Lee: Yes, you are right. And there is one more thing which is important.

Bada Song: What is that?

Dr. Peter Lee: How do you feel when you are singing a song?

Bada Song: I feel happy when I am singing my favorite songs and listening to music.

Dr. Peter Lee: Yes, that is one of the main reasons why many people are listening to music and singing songs. When you keep singing a song, you can memorize its lyrics at the same time. In addition, you can practice your pronunciation as well.

Bada Song: Oh, that is what I am expecting from this method. I am listening to my favorite songs again so that the lyrics of the songs can be remembered with ease. Listening and speaking practice by using a song is one of the best learning methods to enhance my English proficiency.

Dr. Peter Lee: That is why I also used to listen to English songs and follow them.

Bada Song: Would you sing your favorite song for us, please?

Dr. Peter Lee: No. I am embarrassed to sing!

Bada Song: No, we want to hear your song. Please?

Dr. Peter Lee: No. I cannot.

Bada Song: P-L-E-A-S-E!

Dr. Peter Lee: Okay, okay. Then please be patient even if I am not a good singer. Okay?

Bada Song: Okay!

Dr. Peter Lee: *"Wise men say... only fools rush in... but I can't help... falling in love with you... Shall I stay... it would be a sin... but I can't help... falling in love with you."*

Bada Song: What is the title of the song?

Dr. Peter Lee: The title of the song is *Can't Help Falling In Love With You* sung by the late popular singer, Elvis Presley.

Bada Song: Do you like the song?

Dr. Peter Lee: Yes, I like it.

Bada Song: Could you explain the song?

Dr. Peter Lee: Oh, that is a good question. Do you know what the expression *'can't help falling in love with you'* means?

Bada Song: I don't know. What does that mean?

Dr. Peter Lee: It means that wise men think about themselves not falling in love because they probably think about themselves being wise and intelligent, and not overcome by emotions. They think that only fools dash and hurry to love women. However, when a man meets a woman whose personality is exactly what he has been expecting his whole life, there is no way for him to deny his feelings toward the woman – and this is called falling in love!

Bada Song: Oh, that is why he said that he can't help falling in love with a woman.

Dr. Peter Lee: Right. There is no way to resist his affection. *Can't help falling in love with you* means totally the opposite meaning that he loves her so much because she is the only one for his life. Even if he tries to control his feelings, he cannot because he is simply so in love with her. Have you ever had that kind of feeling in your life?

Bada Song: Yes, I have.

Dr. Peter Lee: Really? You are just a university student.

Bada Song: Do you mean that a university student can't help falling in love with somebody?

Dr. Peter Lee: No, what I am telling you is just a joke. But if it is an attempt for you to use the expression that we just discussed, you are using it very well.

Bada Song: Oh, thank you.

Dr. Peter Lee: One more valuable point that we cannot overlook is the discussion of the lyrics of a song.

Discussion is a good method of learning English. Some lyrics written or spoken in a song are profound and vague so that they are a good topic to discuss with each other. Like what we just did. But there is also a weakness in using English songs when you are learning English. We just discussed that some lyrics are vague and profound, so that it is hard to understand clearly the meanings of lyrics. Some song lyrics are also phrased like a poem, and that is why they may not be good examples of correct sentences. I hope that you get all the advantages mentioned above while using English songs.

Bada Song: I see. Thank you so much for helping me to understand the effects of using English songs in learning English.

## Discussion topic 17: Using an English-Korean dictionary

Dr. Peter Lee: Then, let us discuss another topic which is extremely important to every English learner. Someone noted that using an English-Korean dictionary is useful for English learners. Who suggested this?

Gamsa Park: I did.

Dr. Peter Lee: Why don't you explain your suggestion in detail?

Gamsa Park: An English-Korean dictionary is a basic item that every student should have if they want to learn English. Without using an English-Korean dictionary, it would be impossible for me to know the basic meaning of unknown words while reading English articles.

Dr. Peter Lee: Is it really helpful for you to use an English-Korean dictionary?

Gamsa Park: Of course it is! If I don't know the meaning of a word, how can I understand it? If there are many words that I don't know in sentences, I cannot understand the messages of these sentences. If there are many words that I don't know in a book, how can I understand the contents of the book? I think that a word is a basic building block needed in composing in English just as you need bricks to construct a building.

Dr. Peter Lee: I understand what you mean. You're right. A book is composed of many sentences; sentences are composed of many phrases; and the phrases are composed of many words.

If you don't know the meaning of a word in a phrase, you cannot understand the meaning of the phrase. If you don't know the meaning of a phrase, in turn, you cannot understand the meaning of a sentence. Consequently, if you don't know the meaning of a sentence, you cannot understand the meaning of a book. Is this what you are saying?

Gamsa Park: Yes, that is correct.

Dr. Peter Lee: However, it is impossible for you to know the whole of English vocabulary. There are more than 1,000,000 words in English and new words are being made as time goes by. How can you memorize and remember the entirety of English?

Gamsa Park: That is also right.

Dr. Peter Lee: If we had to memorize all English vocabulary, we would always be worried about listening, speaking, reading, and writing in English because there would always be some words that we don't know. However, this is not true. Even though there are some words that you don't know, you can guess the meaning of a sentence. Sometimes, you cannot understand its meaning precisely. However, you can surmise its meaning from the other words in the sentence. Do you know what I am really worried about?

Gamsa Park: I don't know.

Dr. Peter Lee: I am worried about using an English-Korean dictionary.

Gamsa Park: Why?

Dr. Peter Lee: I know that using an English-Korean dictionary is important, but you should also try to use an English-English dictionary.

Gamsa Park: Why? I have never thought about using an English-English dictionary. I just need to check the meaning of a word that I didn't know while studying English. An English-Korean dictionary is a book for helping me to understand the meaning of a word that I don't know. That is enough.

Dr. Peter Lee: No, that is not enough! You said that a sentence is composed of several words. If the sentence is a building, a word is a brick of it. This is what you are saying.

Gamsa Park: Right. Indeed, I said that.

Dr. Peter Lee: What if the building collapses because of bricks?

Gamsa Park: I don't know what you are driving at.

Dr. Peter Lee: Listen carefully! Many students are just using an English-Korean dictionary in order to understand the meaning of a word that they don't know while studying English. Many students also memorize the Korean meanings of English vocabulary.

Gamsa Park: Right.

Dr. Peter Lee: That is the biggest mistake that you have made while studying English for years.

Gamsa Park: Why?

Dr. Peter Lee: Because it is such a big mistake that many students have made! I will clarify the problems that occur when using an English-Korean dictionary. Let me give an example. Do you know the meaning of the word *school*?

Gamsa Park: Of course.

Dr. Peter Lee: Please tell me the meaning of the word.

Gamsa Park: Hakyo (It means school in Korean).

Dr. Peter Lee: Could you explain the meaning of the word *school* in English?

Gamsa Park: …

Dr. Peter Lee: Just try it. You don't need to make a perfect sentence.

Gamsa Park: Students are studying.

Dr. Peter Lee: No, why don't you explain it more?

Gamsa Park: A student goes to study.

Dr. Peter Lee: No. A school is kind of place, right?

Gamsa Park: Right.

Dr. Peter Lee: What kind of place is a school?

Gamsa Park: Students are studying and learning subjects.

Dr. Peter Lee: Yes, you are right. Have you ever learned a relative clause in English class?

Gamsa Park: Yes, of course.

Dr. Peter Lee: Why don't you explain the word school using a relative clause?

Gamsa Park: Okay. A school is a place where students are

learning and studying subjects.

Dr. Peter Lee: What kind of subjects do you learn in school?

Gamsa Park: Korean, English, mathematics, chemistry, and so on.

Dr. Peter Lee: You are right. Why don't you explain school using a full sentence?

Gamsa Park: A school is a place where students are studying and learning subjects such as Korean, English, mathematics, and so on.

Dr. Peter Lee: You did a good job! That is right. You can make English sentences while learning new English words. In addition, you are using the basic knowledge of English grammar. How about that? Is it more interesting to you? Or is just memorizing the Korean meaning of English vocabulary better?

Gamsa Park: I think that it is better to understand English words using English sentences instead of memorizing their Korean meanings.

Dr. Peter Lee: Of course! You and I definitely agree that a word is like a brick, which is a material used to construct a building. If you know English words, how to make a sentence, and the basic knowledge of English grammar, I am sure you will improve your ability in English.

Gamsa Park: Really?

Dr. Peter Lee: It is difficult for you to understand every English word by making English sentences. However, it can be a better option than just memorizing the Korean meaning of an English word.

Gamsa Park: But how can I make an English sentence when my English ability is not good enough to make a perfect sentence in English?

Dr. Peter Lee: That is a good question. You don't need to make an English sentence in order to understand the meaning of English vocabulary.

Gamsa Park: Really? I have heard that using an English-English dictionary is helpful for learning English. But I have not tried it because it seems so difficult.

Dr. Peter Lee: No, it is not difficult. Sometimes, it might be difficult for you to use an English-English dictionary, but you can become more familiar with it as you use it more frequently. There are many benefits that you will experience when you use an English-English dictionary.

Gamsa Park: What are these?

Dr. Peter Lee: Have you ever had to memorize many Korean meanings of one English word written in an English-Korean dictionary?

Gamsa Park: Yes, it is really confusing and I am still asking myself about why there are so many meanings of just one English word!

Dr. Peter Lee: You are right. I had the same feeling too.

Gamsa Park: Actually, I gave up learning English because

there are too many English words that I have to memorize. In addition, English words have various meanings. I was stressed while memorizing a lot of English vocabulary. Thus, I abandoned learning English.

Dr. Peter Lee: How sad a story that is! English mentors must teach English in a practical manner, not in a theoretical way. So many students have studied English since elementary school, but they cannot speak English well. They think that they have to memorize many English words, but they cannot use them properly and effectively. They always try to examine the sentence that they made in a grammatical manner.

You may ask, “What is the basic function of a language?” I say that a language is composed of the words and sounds created in order to communicate with each other. Why do many language learners approach learning foreign languages so seriously? Do they want to become linguists who analyze the structure of languages?

Anyway, let us go back to the point that we were talking about a while ago. An English-Korean dictionary indicates too many Korean meanings of English vocabulary, which could lead to confusion among English learners. The various meanings of English words are useful for translators who translate English sentences into Korean sentences and vice versa. However, too many meanings can be confusing to English learners, especially if they are just beginners.

Gamsa Park: Are you suggesting, then, that we have to use only an English-English dictionary instead of an English-Korean dictionary?

Dr. Peter Lee: Of course not. You need to use both of them. If you still don't understand very well the meaning of English vocabulary by using an English-English dictionary, you can use an English-Korean dictionary. I will explain how to use both an English-Korean dictionary and an English-English dictionary in detail in the second part of my lecture.

Gamsa Park: Oh, thank you!

Dr. Peter Lee: We have been discussing many topics about how to learn English and what is the best way to learn English from various perspectives. There are only two topics remaining on the board. One is about writing English emails to pen pals, while the other one is about talking to each other in English.

## Discussion topic 18: Writing e-mails to a pen pal in English

Dr. Peter Lee: First, let us talk about writing English emails to pen pals. Is this a good way to learn English? Who suggested this?

Dajeong Ham: I did.

Dr. Peter Lee: Why don't you explain it in detail?

Dajeong Ham: Yes, I will. I was born and raised in a rural area where a few people lived. The small town where I lived was really tiny. People in the small town knew each other very well, just like family members. However, I didn't have close friends because most of the residents were older than me. When I was an elementary school student, all the students in the village except me were high school students or university students. There was no way to form a close friendship with anyone whose age was similar to mine.

Dr. Peter Lee: It sounds like you were born and raised in a rural village where people live in remote areas with no electricity or other basic infrastructure.

Dajeong Ham: No way! Why would you think that way about the village where I lived? I had a computer. Other families in the town also had one or two. I lived in just a small village, not in a primitive society, you know?

Dr. Peter Lee: Oh, I am so sorry. I didn't want to underestimate where you were living. I just pictured where you lived from what you said. Anyway, keep going!

Dajeong Ham: Okay. I really wanted to have a friend in order to share interests which young children usually have. However, it was impossible for me to play with anyone after school. In elementary school, I had a lot of friends in my class, but there was no one whose age was the same as mine in the village. That was the problem.

In addition, I wanted to meet many friends, including foreign ones. When I watched TV, dramas, or movies, many people in the programs had different skin colors, different languages, different cultures, and different lifestyles. That was extremely interesting to me.

Dr. Peter Lee: What did you do in order to solve your problems?

Dajeong Ham: I drank a cup of coffee. Do you know *Americano*?

Dr. Peter Lee: Yes, I know. But you should not have drunk it because you were just an elementary school student at the time.

Dajeong Ham: I am just joking. I just wanted to say that I didn't live in a primitive village.

Dr. Peter Lee: Oh, don't joke any more. So what did you do?

Dajeong Ham: I had a computer hooked up to the Internet. I had access to the Internet and found communities which were involved with many foreign friends. It was just a starting point to making friends around the world from a tiny village. Through the Internet, I could go anywhere and everywhere, anytime I wished, with no time limit.

Dr. Peter Lee: Oh, I see. So you kept sending out emails in English?

Dajeong Ham: Yes, I did! I met an American friend on the Internet whose name was Peter, just like you. He was an elementary school kid. We sent a lot of e-mails back and forth. Through that activity, I learned a lot of English words and expressions. It was fun, even though I had to study English harder in order to explain what I wanted to say to my friend Peter. I opened an English dictionary which was too big and thick for my little hands, but I had to. I opened it thousands of times to find proper words and expressions. The dictionary that I used remains on my desk at home. When I look at it, I am always reminded of that memory, which was so precious during my pen pal experience.

Dr. Peter Lee: Is Peter still your friend?

Dajeong Ham: Not anymore. I hope that you will become my friend, sir?

Dr. Peter Lee: Okay. But you must be polite and not joke around anymore.

Dajeong Ham: Yes, sir!

Dr. Peter Lee: Oh, now I was joking. Anyway, we finally have left only one topic to talk about on what is the best way to learn English.

## Discussion topic 19: Talking to each other in English

Dr. Peter Lee: Who wrote on the board that talking to each other in English is a good method of learning English?

Mideum Mal: I did.

Dr. Peter Lee: Would you please explain it in more detail? Oh, wait a second. Your last name is one that I have never heard of in Korea.

Mideum Mal: Do you know my first name?

Dr. Peter Lee: No.

Mideum Mal: Mideum.

Dr. Peter Lee: So your full name is Mal Mideum, in the Korean name-order?

Mideum Mal: Yes. My name is also Mideum Mal in English name-order. Name-order in Korean and English is actually opposite. The surname is first and the given name is last in Korean; in English, the surname is last and the given name is first.

Dr. Peter Lee: You are right. Anyway, why do you think that talking to each other in English is the best way to learn English?

Mideum Mal: I don't know about English grammar and I don't know many English words as well. I am just a simple person. What I mean to say is that I just talk to foreign people when they are asking about basic things, such as directions to their destination, cultural information, and so on. You might meet foreigners on the street, asking you about destinations. I have also met foreigners on the street. I used to avoid talking to them even though they ask me for particular directions. I was a very shy person who was nervous and uncomfortable while encountering foreigners on the street or even Koreans who are not known to me. I was extremely nervous when I encountered foreigners. However, they asked me simple questions and I gave them answers using simple and easy words.

Dr. Peter Lee: Did they understand your explanation?

Mideum Mal: Partly, yes. Some foreigners understood and some foreigners didn't understand. However, it was an amazing experience which made me feel confident. Do you know why?

Dr. Peter Lee: No, I don't know. Tell us why.

Mideum Mal: I felt very good because they expressed their gratitude to me for giving an answer to their question. In addition, I was becoming more confident as I met more foreigners.

Dr. Peter Lee: Really? Why?

Mideum Mal: Actually, I could not speak English well and I didn't know about English grammar and many English words. But I could talk to foreigners using simple English words.

For example, I used the following words *"go, come, turn, up, down, right, and left,"* for letting them know particular directions. Are they difficult English words? Definitely not! Foreigners ask me *"Does the bus go to City Hall?"* Then, I tell them *"Yes or no"*.

Foreigners usually ask me by using simple words and I answer them using simple words as well. I am glad because this means I have more chances to meet foreigners on the street and more chances for me to speak English.

Dr. Peter Lee: You are right. But I think that you have not had any chances to talk to foreigners whom you meet on the street about serious topics. Have you?

Mideum Mal: No, I have not. I like talking to people in Korean and I also enjoy talking to foreigners in English after accumulating more experiences as time passes. But it isn't easy to meet and talk in English to foreigners on the street. Now, I am voluntarily approaching them and saying "Hi" in order to talk to them in English. But I don't want to do it anymore.

Dr. Peter Lee: Why?

Mideum Mal: I really want to talk more in English.

Dr. Peter Lee: Then, why don't you try other ways?

Mideum Mal: How?

Dr. Peter Lee: Do you think that you can develop your ability to speak in English only by meeting foreigners?

Mideum Mal: I think so. I think it would be very weird to talk to Koreans in English. Of course, I have never talked to Koreans in English.

Dr. Peter Lee: Why not?

Mideum Mal: Koreans use the Korean language in order to communicate with each other. In addition, I am not good at

English and they are not also good English speakers. Our speaking may be a kind of *Konglish*. *Konglish* means that Koreans speak English in Korean ways. Native speakers whose mother tongue is English encounter difficulty in understanding *Konglish*. They probably understand *Konglish* but they know that *Konglish* expressions are not correct English. I will give you an example to describe what a *Konglish* expression is.

A waitress appears and asks. *'Are you ready to order?'* Then, someone who is speaking *Konglish* might say, *'I am coffee.'* Do you know what I mean? The waitress understands what he wants to have but it is not a correct English expression.

Dr. Peter Lee: Do you always want to make correct expressions in English? What if your English expressions are not exactly correct when you are conversing with foreigners in English? Do you expect that your English sentences and expressions are always perfect?

Mideum Mal: No.

Dr. Peter Lee: Do you think that you could make more correct sentences in English if you talked only to native English speakers?

Mideum Mal: No. But I could learn correct and natural English expressions from them.

Dr. Peter Lee: Yes, that is one of the benefits gained from conversations with English native speakers. However, you can also make correct and natural sentences and expressions from dialogue with your Korean colleagues.

Mideum Mal: How?

Dr. Peter Lee: You use many English textbooks which actually include a lot of dialogue useful in many situations. Make an appointment with your friend and practice English dialogues every day. Would that be difficult?

Mideum Mal: No.

Dr. Peter Lee: What about talking to your Korean friends in English, even though you and your Korean friends are not good at speaking English?

Mideum Mal: Our English sentences may all be wrong.

Dr. Peter Lee: I don't care about whether the English sentences that you express are right or wrong. The most important thing is that your *Konglish* sentences and expressions are going to become correct and natural English sentences and expressions.

Mideum Mal: Really?

Dr. Peter Lee: Yes, definitely. But you need to choose some specific topics in order to talk to your Korean friends in English. Do you know that your speech, based on whatever topics, is actually going to be a discussion?

Mideum Mal: Really?

Dr. Peter Lee: Of course. While discussing various topics with your Korean friends in English, you will be making a great effort to find proper words and expressions in your brain. That is the way to improve your English speaking. It does not matter whether you are talking to Koreans or native English speakers.

The most important thing is that you get better at speaking English when you open your mouth to talk using that language.

Mideum Mal: Really?

Dr. Peter Lee: I have already discussed many issues pertinent to English education in the first part of my lecture. All the students here in my class discussed their respective methods for learning English. And we have discussed whether their recommendations are right or wrong in order to figure out the most trustworthy methods of learning English. Through a lot of discussion, we have found advantages and disadvantages to individual English learning methods. Through a lot of discussion, I have eliminated unnecessary ways to learn English. Students suggested a lot of English learning methods and I dismissed some of those which were non-essential. I kept asking about many questions to you in this class. Do you know why?

Students in the class: No.

Dr. Peter Lee: This is my teaching strategy, in which I aim to discover the right way to learn English while eliminating a lot of wrong ways. Eliminating a lot of wrong ways means that your success rate in learning English rises, by reducing many errors, which come from wrong ways of learning English. After our long discussion you can now understand the wrong ways of learning English. Therefore, it is time for you to know the right way to learn English. Do you want to start a journey with me in order to discover the right way of learning English? This journey is neither difficult nor easy. However, it is worthy.

Students in the class: If there is a right way to learn English, I would like to learn it.

Dr. Peter Lee: Do you really want to learn it?

Students in the class: Yes, we really want to learn it.

Dr. Peter Lee: But I think that, unfortunately, about thirty percent among you here will probably give up learning English after my instruction.

Students in the class: Why?

Dr. Peter Lee: In my past teaching experience, some students didn't follow my teaching. Probably, they were not interested in my teaching.

Each student: That would not be me.

Dr. Peter Lee: Alright. Let us start a new journey which is called *'The Resurrection of English Education'*. Before this journey, I want to share my favorite poem, *The Road Not Taken*, by Robert Frost.

*Two roads diverged in a wood, and I took the one less traveled by, and that has made all the difference.*

Are you ready to start a new journey *The Resurrection of English Education*?

All students in the class: Yes, we are ready!

Dr. Peter Lee: Let's go and start a new way of learning English!

# PART TWO

## RENEWING ENGLISH LEARNING ACTIVITIES

# 3

## The chief cornerstone in English learning activities

The stone which the builders rejected has become the chief cornerstone (Matthew 21:42).

Dr. Peter Lee: We discussed a lot of English learning methods in the first part of this class. There were a lot of discussions about many controversial issues on how to learn English from various perspectives. Why did we discuss English learning methods with me and your colleagues in this class?

Seongsil Park: To share our opinions.

Dr. Peter Lee: Yes, you are right! But the most important reason is to discuss with each other a conclusive way to learn English correctly. In addition, wrong and unreliable methods must be eliminated as soon as you discover the right and wrong ways to learn English.

Seongsil Park: In the last part of the first session in class I learned something.

Dr. Peter Lee: What is that?

Seongsil Park: I used to follow the ways that many people took. However, in the case of English learning methods, I must examine whether the ways that many people follow are right or wrong.

Dr. Peter Lee: You are definitely right! That is what I really expect from you. You are not a kid anymore. Thus, you have to decide what the right path is in order to be able to follow it.

Seongsil Park: However, how can I know whether the way that I am taking is right or wrong?

Dr. Peter Lee: That is a good question. Now you are totally different. In the past, you were just following an English learning method that many people did, without any effort to analyze whether it was right or wrong. However, you are asking me about how you can know the right or wrong way of learning English. Please keep asking me any question pertinent to English learning methods and discover the right ways of learning English. I am sure that the way that I am going to introduce these methods is one of the best ways for you, so as not to waste your time, which is invaluable.

Seongsil Park: Thank you so much for introducing us to the right way of learning English. But I really want to know how I can find out the right way of learning English.

Dr. Peter Lee: There are many ways to discover the right methods to learn English. For example, we discussed a lot with our colleagues in order to find out the right ways to learn English. And we eliminated some unnecessary ways and agreed with each other about some specific methods of learning English. However, you are unable to decide on your own the best way to learn English. Do you know why?

Seongsil Park: No, why?

Dr. Peter Lee: Because you don't know what is the right or wrong way to learn English. Thus, you need a mentor or a teacher who will help you discover the right way of learning English.

Seongsil Park: Mentors?

Dr. Peter Lee: Do you know what a mentor means?

Seongsil Park: A mentor is a person who helps someone and gives them advice.

Dr. Peter Lee: Yes, exactly right! From now on, I would like to become a mentor for all of you here in this class who are listening to my lecture. You are here to learn English. This is the common goal that students here have in mind. You are going to hear important information about English. I will give you the exact same information. However, some will accept my advice while others will reject it. Some will agree with my opinion while others will disagree. Some of you are going to be changed by my lectures and some in this class will not be changed. I am not warning you, but I am telling you the truth. From my own teaching experience, approximately seventy percent of students will succeed and the rest, or thirty percent, will fail.

Seongsil Park: May I ask what the reason is?

Dr. Peter Lee: There are several reasons. I am telling you some specific reasons which led the other thirty percent of students in my class to fail.

Seongsil Park: Do we have to discuss them as well?

Dr. Peter Lee: Of course. In my class, I discuss all relevant ideas with my students. I always think that teaching is an interactive relationship between students and teachers. If I am teaching something, students should also be thinking about the ideas and eventually accept them. In fact, I will try to listen to your opinions and share our thoughts in order to discover a method which may be complete.

Somang Kim: Do you think that there is such a thing as something complete?

Dr. Peter Lee: Nothing may be complete. However, it is possible to reduce failure while increasing success rates. I have asked students often about why they give up learning English and many students said that they are not good at English. It means that they have no talent for learning English. Sometimes, students don't like English. I also don't want to force them to learn English. But I am worried that many students don't realize that they may actually have potentials or a bright future in learning good English. Let me ask one question.

Somang Kim: What is it?

Dr. Peter Lee: Do you think that learning English has been easy or difficult as you have progressed? Would you please raise your hand, if you feel learning English has been easy as you have learned it more?

Students in the class: (No one raises his/her hand!)

Dr. Peter Lee: Oh my goodness!

Students: English is difficult!

Dr. Peter Lee: Why is it difficult?

Somang Kim: Because English grammar is difficult and there are too many words to memorize.

Dr. Peter Lee: You have been learning English for more than ten years and you probably know many words and have knowledge of English grammar. It means that you are much better off than others because you have studied English vocabulary and English grammar.

Somang Kim: Your statement is logical.

Dr. Peter Lee: You mean that my statement is logical but you cannot accept it.

Somang Kim: I could accept it, if you explain it more clearly.

Dr. Peter Lee: I see what you mean. I think it would be better for you and other students here to understand what I mean to say.

Somang Kim: Please explain it in a simpler way.

Dr. Peter Lee: Alright. You have been learning English grammar and memorizing a lot of English vocabulary. You have taken a lot of English classes in school and in private classes.

Many students might have taken English classes in English institutes. Normally, students have been studying English since elementary school. It means that they have been studying English for more than ten years. However, you feel that English is difficult. Many students cannot speak English well and hesitate to make English sentences. Why? Why can't you speak English well?

Somang Kim: I don't know. I really don't know.

Dr. Peter Lee: The reason for the feeling that English is difficult is that you have been learning English in totally opposite ways.

Somang Kim: Totally opposite ways?

Dr. Peter Lee: Yes, you have been learning English the wrong way.

Somang Kim: That is a frightening word because it means that my efforts are futile.

Dr. Peter Lee: No, I never said that. You can fix it if you want. Don't speak negatively! Do you know the meaning of the word RESURRECTION?

Somang Kim: Resurrection means someone lives again after death.

Dr. Peter Lee: Yes, you are right! Your English ability can be resurrected by a new training method for learning English. Your English ability can be strengthened and made more concrete. All the information that you have will be useful and fruitful if you are trained from the base of learning English.

Somang Kim: From the base of learning English?

Dr. Peter Lee: Yes. In order to understand the base of learning English, you have to know the correct answer to the following question.

Somang Kim: Another question? You are asking me too many questions!

Dr. Peter Lee: I am asking many questions in order to find the right solutions to the problems that you have had in learning English. What is the right step to learn English among listening, speaking, reading, and writing? What is the first, second, third, and fourth step?

Somang Kim: Maybe the first step is speaking.

Dr. Peter Lee: Why?

Somang Kim: I think that speaking is the most important thing among them.

Dr. Peter Lee: That is very interesting. Okay, I am going to change the question. What do you think is the first that you learn among listening, speaking, reading, and writing when you want to be proficient in Korean?

Somang Kim: Maybe listening?

Dr. Peter Lee: Now you are thinking about the language learning process correctly!

You are correct that you learn listening first when you are learning Korean. When your mother was pregnant, she might have said, *"I love you, my pretty one and I love you more than anyone."*

After she gave birth and you came out to this beautiful world, she was very happy. She probably hugged you, kissed you, and sang for you all day long. You could not understand what your mother was saying to you but you listened to it every day and every night. When you finally said one or two words like *mama*, your mother was very happy, even if you could not know exactly what the word meant. When you were two or three years old, you made some weird sentences which were imperfect and incomplete. The sentences you spoke were composed of a few words, but your father and mother understood what you meant. Do you imagine that this is the whole process of learning Korean?

Somang Kim: Yes, I think so. I cannot identify what I did when I was very young, like one or two years old. However, your statement is definitely right because nobody can say a word without listening. I mean, there is nobody who can speak without listening to any words in their life. Without listening to Korean, it would be impossible for me to speak Korean. Just imagine a situation where I never heard any Korean language in my whole life because I was deaf. Then, how could I ever speak Korean?

Dr. Peter Lee: Yes, yes, yes! That is what I was talking about! Now, it is time for you to think about your English learning process. Did you start learning English from listening?

Somang Kim: No.

Dr. Peter Lee: Why?

Somang Kim: I don't know. Nobody told me that I had to listen to English if I wanted to learn English at the beginning of the process.

Dr. Peter Lee: Now, you completely understand what I am talking about. You have to fix your English learning process.

Somang Kim: How?

Dr. Peter Lee: Listen to English!

Students in the class: (Quiet)

Dr. Peter Lee: Now, you need to ask me any question related to what I just said, *"listen to English."*

Gamdong Min: What do I have to listen to?

Dr. Peter Lee: Oh, now you are asking me the right question. Yes, that is right. You have to ask me what you have to listen to. You have to choose the right listening material.

Gamdong Min: The right listening material?

Dr. Peter Lee: Please don't choose a listening material which is much higher than your English ability.

Gamdong Min: Would you please explain it in more detail? I don't understand it clearly.

Dr. Peter Lee: Of course. If you want to select an appropriate listening tape for yourself, you have to choose one which you can understand seventy percent.

Gamdong Min: About seventy percent?

Dr. Peter Lee: Yes, understanding about seventy percent of an English tape means that you can generally follow what people are saying in that tape.

Gamdong Min: Generally?

Dr. Peter Lee: Yes, generally understanding an English tape means that you can understand the overall story of its content with the exception of some specific details.

Gamdong Min: Now, I understand what you mean.

Dr. Peter Lee: I cannot calculate the precise percentage even though I told you about seventy percent. But that is a guideline to choosing the right English tape for you. The seventy percent standard means this – if you are having difficulty in listening to an English tape that you chose, that is not the right tape for you. If you feel that an English tape that you chose is too easy for you to understand, then that is not the correct tape for you either. However, when you are listening to an English tape and you can generally understand what people are saying in it, then the tape might be right for you. Do you understand what I mean?

Gamdong Min: Yes, I understand what you mean. Is there any other criteria for choosing the right English tape for me?

Dr. Peter Lee: The second thing that you have to consider when you are choosing the right English tape is the speed of it.

Gamdong Min: The speed of an English tape?

Dr. Peter Lee: Yes. Please don't choose an English tape which is spoken too slow or too fast. You have to choose an English tape which is spoken normally.

In addition, don't choose an English tape which is comprised of both Korean and English. That is really dangerous. Your English learning process may be ruined if you choose English tapes which are recorded both in Korean and English.

Gamdong Min: Really?

Dr. Peter Lee: Of course. Do you think that I am lying?

Gamdong Min: No.

Dr. Peter Lee: I am sorry that I am too serious. But you must avoid English tapes recorded in both Korean and English. Do you know how extremely important the English-listening learning process is? This is the first step to creating the English structure in your brain.

Gamdong Min: The English structure of my brain?

Dr. Peter Lee: Yes. It may be difficult for you to understand. The structure of something means the way in which it is specifically organized. Each language has its particular structure. Let's think about Korean. The order of the words in a Korean sentence is the following: a subject is written first, then, the object in the middle, and a verb is written last. Meanwhile, the order of an English sentence is that a subject is first, a verb is in the middle, and an object is last. In English, it is correct to say, *"I go to school"* and it is wrong to say, *"I school to go."* This is a brief explanation of the disparity between the structure of

Korean and English. Can you understand what I mean?

Gamdong Min: I understand what you mean. Do you think that the structure of a language is important? If yes, why?

Dr. Peter Lee: Yes, the structure of a language is definitely significant in learning languages. When I tell you the word *structure*, you may not understand it fully. So, I will try to explain the word *structure* using another word: pattern.

When you are listening to songs over and over, the song that you have listened to may become very familiar to your ears. Thus, you can sing along without difficulty. Have you experienced this before?

Gamdong Min: Of course! I really like songs, thus, I usually listen to my favorite songs while going to school.

Dr. Peter Lee: Do you always check the lyrics of songs you sing most often?

Gamdong Min: No. I just sing along after listening to it many times. I can also guess the next lyrics as they are sung. It is because I am already familiar with the lyrics because of listening to it repeatedly.

Dr. Peter Lee: Yes, you are right. Indeed, the reason is that you become familiar with the song when you repeat it. In addition, you can become very accustomed to the pattern of the song as you listen to it continually. I cannot say it as a theory because I have not proven it scientifically. However, nobody can deny that people can follow the lyrics of a song after listening to it over and over, even without checking the lyrics. People who have the same language can easily memorize a song whose lyrics are in their native language, especially, when they listen to the song over and over. Have you ever found people who use a totally different language structure in your society? Or have you ever discovered people whose language structure is absolutely different from yours, even though their mother tongue is the same?

Gamdong Min: No. If there is that kind of person, he or she is not a normal person, but probably a crazy one.

Dr. Peter Lee: You are exactly right. There is nobody who has a different language structure if their mother tongue is the same. However, there are many people who have different language structures when they are learning a foreign language.

Sarang Park: Really?

Dr. Peter Lee: You can probably discover this for yourself.

Sarang Park: Really? I don't know what you are talking about.

Dr. Peter Lee: You might be someone who speaks a different pattern or structure of English compared to that of English native speakers.

Sarang Park: Me?

Dr. Peter Lee: Not only you but also your colleagues here in this class.

Sarang Park: Really?

Dr. Peter Lee: That is correct! Many students may think that your English is not correct, but is a type of *Konglish*. Konglish is English, but spoken in the Korean way. It means that your English speaking pattern or structure is not expressed following the basic principles of clear and effective English. Do you know why?

Sarang Park: I don't know.

Dr. Peter Lee: There is a definite reason. You feel that your English is not English but *Konglish* because you have ignored how important LISTENING practice is in learning English. Many students here have not practiced English listening. They just think that they can select the correct answer on English listening examinations. If their listening score is higher than what they expected, probably, they were just lucky. You must discard this kind of thinking.

Sarang Park: Don't be angry, sir.

Dr. Peter Lee: I am not angry with you but I really emphasize how important listening practice is in learning English. Okay, let me tell you another thing which is tremendously important.

If you really want to learn English, you must listen to English conversations and spend a lot of time practicing your listening skills. If you underestimate how important listening practice is in learning English, you may not get your expected scores on English examinations or obtain the good results that you hope for.

Sarang Park: But I haven't spent time on English listening

practice. When I took English exams, including twenty listening questions out of fifty, I thought that I might get lucky and do better than expected. Do you know why?

Dr. Peter Lee: I guess so. You didn't know how to prepare for English listening exams. In addition, you couldn't even try to prepare for English listening exams because you didn't know from where you had to study.

Sarang Park: Yes, that is right. I never even knew what kind of English textbook I had to use for an English listening examination. I think that the range of English listening exams is too broad for me to prepare.

Dr. Peter Lee: That is why you probably spent a lot of time studying English grammar or reading tests rather than English listening exams. Is that right?

Sarang Park: Yes, you are right. Preparing English listening exams is sort of like discovering a coin covered by sand in a desert. Random chance! I don't know how and what to prepare for English listening examinations.

Dr. Peter Lee: Thank you so much for sharing your problem. But you must remember that English listening is the first and most basic step in learning English. This rule never changes over time! This is the truth about learning English. Others say that there are two sections relevant to English learning. One section is on listening and speaking while the other section is reading and writing. Thus, someone might say that it is difficult for us to learn two different sections simultaneously. Do you think that that concept is true?

Sarang Park: I don't know.

Dr. Peter Lee: Of course that is not true. If you are listening to English and speaking English well, you should also be able to read and write it well. In the case of technical and professional papers such as journal articles or dissertations, writing skills should match with listening, speaking, and reading skills. Writing skills should be trained by specific methods. Anyway, that is not the point here. The point that I am emphasizing is that you must remember how important listening practice is in learning English.

Sarang Park: Do you think that there is no other way to start learning English than listening practice?

Dr. Peter Lee: Of course! There is no other way but listening practice because it is the most important basic step for every foreign language learner.

IF YOU DON'T WANT TO LISTEN TO ENGLISH, DO NOT LEARN ENGLISH!

Sarang Park: That sentence makes me frightened and frustrated.

Dr. Peter Lee: Why?

Sarang Park: Because I have never done English listening practice since I started learning English. Your testimony made me feel that I have wasted my English learning time in my life.

Dr. Peter Lee: No, don't be so negative. Cheer up! Don't forsake what you have initially learned and your potential which is kind of like *a mustard seed planted in your soul.* I would like to share this sentence written in the Bible.

*"Though your beginning was small, yet your latter end would increase abundantly (Job 8:7)."*

Your starting point of learning English is listening. You must start to listen to English from now on. You must!

Sarang Park: How long do I have to listen to English and until when do I have to listen to it?

Dr. Peter Lee: There is no graduation day for finishing English listening practice. However, I guarantee that you will like listening to English. Let us imagine that you will understand what English speakers are saying in a movie without subtitles translated from English into Korean. You will be very happy when you understand what English native speakers are saying to you in English. In addition, during conversations, you are responding to them in English in which your English expressions are precisely correct.

Sarang Park: Really?

Dr. Peter Lee: Can you imagine this? For example, English native speakers are talking to their companions on the street and you are just passing by them and you understand what they are talking about. In a train, English native speakers ask you what the next stop is and you tell them the name of the next stop. And you also say to them something like *'Have a nice trip'* when they take off.

Sarang Park: Awesome!

Dr. Peter Lee: You may not believe this. However, if you trust my teaching method, your English ability will flourish.

Gamsa Yang: What does *flourish* mean?

Dr. Peter Lee: *Flourish* means growing and developing quickly.

Gamsa Yang: Do you mean that my English ability will improve quickly if I practice English listening?

Dr. Peter Lee: Yes, that is right. However, you need to be patient. There are many advantages that you may gain from English listening practice. There are so many benefits if you are listening to English well. Of course, you need to be patient for a long period of time in order to develop your listening skill. However, as you know, some say *"No pain, no gain!"* You need time to wait until your English ability, particularly listening, develops and improves.

Gamsa Yang: How long do I have to wait? How many hours do I have to spend listening to English every day?

Dr. Peter Lee: Hold on! I know that you are passionate about learning. But I will respond to your questions one by one, okay?

# 4

## How to improve your English listening ability

Dr. Peter Lee: The first question is how long do you have to wait in order to quickly develop your English ability? First, you have to listen to what I am saying with patience in order to understand the answer to your question. Are you ready?

Students: Yes, we are ready to listen to your instructions.

Dr. Peter Lee: Thank you. I mentioned above that you have to select English tapes which are spoken only in English. And you also have to choose an English tape of which you can understand about seventy percent. After finishing these steps, you have to listen to the English tape you selected. How long do you have to wait in order to improve your English ability in terms of listening skills? You have to listen to it from beginning to end every day, except Sunday.

Gamsa Yang: How long do I have to listen to it per day?

Dr. Peter Lee: That is a good question. I think that you need to spend at least one hour learning English every day.

Gamsa Yang: Only one hour? Is it enough to learn English?

Dr. Peter Lee: If you want to spend more, you could spend two hours every day except Sunday.

Gamsa Yang: Why not Sunday?

Dr. Peter Lee: Sunday is a day that you must take a rest and not do anything. You need to rest as your brain also needs it. I will explain it more in detail later. But you have to spend at least an hour every day learning English. It is not important how many hours you study English, but how you concentrate on learning English. Not quantity but quality! Do you understand what I mean?

Gamsa Yang: Yes. Please explain it more.

Dr. Peter Lee: You have to divide an hour like this: one hour is comprised of sixty minutes and you have to spend thirty minutes listening to the chosen English tape. If your tape is forty minutes long on both the front and the back, then you listen to only the front part of it. Or if you want to listen to the front and the back side of it, that is also fine. This is the first step in English listening practice.

Gamsa Yang: And then? How long do I have to listen to it and until when do I have to listen to it?

Dr. Peter Lee: You have to listen to it over and over until you generally know the whole story. The rule-of-thumb number of times anyone should listen one English tape is one hundred times.

Gamsa Yang: One hundred times!

Dr. Peter Lee: Yes! You have to listen to the same English tape one hundred times. Of course, this calculation can also be applied to the beginner in learning English as a foreign language. If you spend two hours every day, except Sunday, you may go through it three times. But I don't want to recommend listening to it three times, but twice would be much better. If you don't have enough time to listen to it, it would also be fine to listen to it only once a day. However, you must follow the rule that you have to listen to it every day. I have seen so many cases when the rule is broken. Students try to change the rule just like that. They decide to listen to the tape for only one day. In addition, they listen to the tape only for ten times, not one hundred times. Don't do that!

Gamsa Yang: Why not? What is the difference between listening to the tape for one hour every day a week and listening to the tape for six hours but for only one day a week?

If I listen to the tape for an hour each day (except Sunday) for one week, the total number of hours that I listen to it is six hours. If I listen to the tape for six hours but for only one day a week, the total number of hours that I listen to it is THE SAME at six hours per week.

Dr. Peter Lee: No, that is not the same. Not only in language but also in any kind of studies, you cannot study for only one day. This is especially true for learning a language since it is a time-consuming process. For example, I tested you in the first part of this class by using the sentence *'I should've done it.'* You could not understand what the sentence was because you didn't know the sound "V." But now, you know all the sounds of the vowels and consonants because I taught you the "V" sound. In addition, you heard the sentence several times and now you understand the difference between a "V" sound and a "B" sound. This is the process for developing English listening skills.

Gamsa Yang: I see what you mean. Then, why did you talk about *flourish*, which indicates growing quickly?

Dr. Peter Lee: Wait a second! I will explain everything that you want to know. But please listen! If you select one English tape on the basis of your English level, you have to listen to it for one or two hours a day except Sunday. Do you understand clearly what I mean up to this point?

Students: Yes, we do.

Dr. Peter Lee: How many times will you have to listen to the tape in order to finish one English tape?

Students: A hundred times!

Dr. Peter Lee: Yes, you are right. Actually there is no fixed number to listen to one English tape, but you must listen to it until you are following along with the sounds that you hear. In addition, when all the sounds, including intonations, accents, and rhymes, are familiar to your ears, that is the time to stop listening to it. That is why I explained this listening process using a song and its lyrics before.

Somang Kim: I understand what you mean.

Dr. Peter Lee: After you have listened to a thirty-minute English tape until you are familiar with all the sounds spoken in the tape, you can finally go to the next step.

Somang Kim: The next step?

Dr. Peter Lee: Yes, the next step is tremendously important in enhancing English listening skills. It is very relevant in improving your English ability.

Somang Kim: Okay, we are patient and my character is changing. I used to be impatient but now I am getting better.

Dr. Peter Lee: That is a good change. You know that you must be patient if you want to learn not only English but also any other academic knowledge.

Somang Kim: I see. Would you please keep explaining the next step?

Dr. Peter Lee: If you want to know the next step you have to understand the following poem, *The Road Not Taken*, written by Robert Frost. It goes this way:

*Two roads diverged in a wood, and I took the one less traveled by, and that has made all the difference.*

Somang Kim: Is there a clue to discovering the next step?

Dr. Peter Lee: Yes, there is a clue. But I am not pushing you to be patient at this point. What did you do when you were learning Korean in the first year of elementary school?

Somang Kim: I cannot remember.

Dr. Peter Lee: Please try to remember what you did in a Korean language class.

Somang Kim: A teacher read a Korean textbook aloud and we followed reading it aloud.

Dr. Peter Lee: And then what did you do?

Somang Kim: A teacher asked us to write down the Korean words in our notebooks while he read them aloud.

Dr. Peter Lee: You mean dictation, right?

Somang Kim: Yes, we wrote down Korean words and sentences which were spoken aloud by a teacher. Up to now, I still don't know why we had to take dictation.

Dr. Peter Lee: You had not heard any information about how important dictation was from your teacher, but you did it.

Somang Kim: A teacher didn't explain why dictation was important in learning Korean in a Korean class.

Dr. Peter Lee: Have you ever taken dictation in any other academic class except a language class?

Somang Kim: No, I haven't.

Dr. Peter Lee: That is kind of evidence that taking dictation is important, especially in a language class. Why is it important?

Somang Kim: As you said earlier in the first session of this class, taking dictation is related to English listening practice. I think that taking dictation is one of the most effective ways for developing English listening skills.

Dr. Peter Lee: Yes, you are right. But I need you to explain it more precisely.

Somang Kim: I really don't know.

Dr. Peter Lee: Okay, I will explain in detail how important dictation is in English listening practice. Taking dictation is the best way to quickly enhance your English listening skills. You can identify whether the sounds that you are listening to are the same as the letters you wrote. As I mentioned earlier, you must match the sounds and their letters while doing English listening practice. In particular, Koreans must follow this learning process. This is one of the hard and painful activities for developing English listening skills that every English learner must go through.

Somang Kim: Please don't frighten me.

Dr. Peter Lee: No, I don't want you to be frightened by my teaching. However, I am sure that taking dictation is not an easy process for English learners. Owing to its hardship, many English learners ignore this process. Taking dictation is the best way for English learners to identify what kind of sound matches the letters they hear. English learners at the beginning make many mistakes because they have never taken English dictation. Many Korean students make common mistakes while taking dictation because of unaccustomed alphabetical sounds such as F, V, TH, and L sounds. Now, I want you to do something. Please write down this sentence while I am reading it aloud:

*I definitely believe that the faith you have in your mind and in your heart can make your life victorious!*

(Students write it down in a notebook.)

Did you finish writing down the sentence which I read it aloud?

Students in the class: Yes, we did.

Dr. Peter Lee: Actually, it was not a difficult sentence. You probably wrote it down well because all the English words in the sentence are familiar to you. I am going to read it aloud and please read it aloud after me.

*I definitely believe that the faith you have in your mind and in your heart can make your life victorious!*

Students in the class: *I definitely believe that the faith you have in you mind and in your heart can make your life victorious!*

Dr. Peter Lee: One more time!

*I definitely believe that the faith you have in your mind and in your heart can make your life victorious!*

Students in the class: *I definitely believe that the faith you have in your mind and in your heart can make your life victorious!*

Dr. Peter Lee: Sounds good! I really like the use of positive thinking and optimistic words. However, your sounds are not the same as the words in the sentence.

Students in the class: Really?

Dr. Peter Lee: Yes, your sounds are not clear and well-enunciated. If English native speakers listened to your sounds while taking dictation, some of them could not write down the words because of the weird sounds that they hear.

Students: Really?

Dr. Peter Lee: Seriously! I don't want to discourage some of you here but I hope to teach the correct English pronunciation. Miso Han, would you read it aloud after listening to my reading?

Miso Han: Yes, I will.

Dr. Peter Lee: *I definitely believe that the faith that you have in your mind and in your heart can make your life victorious!*

Miso Han: *I definitely believe that the faith that you have in your mind and in your heart can make your life victorious!*

Dr. Peter Lee: No, your sounds are not the same as mine. I don't care about intonation and accent. But I do care about pronunciation.

Miso Han: I don't get it. What is wrong with my speaking?

Dr. Peter Lee: The following words that you said, namely: *DEFINITELY, BELIEVE, THAT, THE, FAITH, HAVE, LIFE,* and *VICTORIOUS* are not the right English pronunciations. Please listen to the sound which is spoken by me. *I definitely believe that the faith that you have in your mind and in your heart can make your life victorious!*

Miso Han: *I definitely believe that the faith that you have in your mind and in your heart can make your life victorious!*

(After Miso Han has read the sentence aloud more than twenty times, that is, after listening to the sounds which were spoken by

Dr. Peter Lee…)

Dr. Peter Lee: Now, your sound and mine are similar. Do you know why?

Miso Han: I just listened to your sound carefully.

Dr. Peter Lee: What you did is a correct method of learning English which involves listening to the sounds repetitively. If you listen to the sound correctly, you can make your sound correctly as well. At the beginning, you didn't make the right sounds such as F and L in the word *definitely*, L and V in the word *believe*, TH in the word *that*, TH in the word *the*, F and TH in the word *faith*, V in the word *have*, L in the word *life*, and V in the word *victorious*. But now, you pronounce the sentence almost correctly.

Miso Han: Almost correctly?

Dr. Peter Lee: Yes, you need to practice saying the correct English pronunciation. You also need to know how to say English vocabulary correctly before pronouncing it. The sentence that we practiced was a little bit long. Let us practice pronouncing with a shorter English sentence. Please read the word THINK aloud.

(Some students pronounce THINK and some students pronounce SINK.)

Dr. Peter Lee: No, that is not right. Not SINK but THINK! Wait a minute! In general, many students here have studied English for more than ten years but some of you are pronouncing it SINK not THINK. Read aloud 'I THINK'!

Some students in the class: *I SINK!*

Dr. Peter Lee: That is the problem. You should've learned how to pronounce English vocabulary. Even though you have learned English grammar and a lot of English vocabulary, you cannot pronounce English vocabulary correctly. You have seen and heard the word *think* a million times but you don't know how to pronounce it correctly. That is the fundamental problem that you have in learning English. Do you want to listen to English well? Then, you must listen to English over and over. Do you want to speak English well? Please speak English more frequently. That is a very simple theory and you don't need to analyze whether this simple theory is right or wrong.

Miso Han: I have been studying English on the wrong track!

Dr. Peter Lee: Now, it is time to fix your problem. That is why I told you the poem *The Road Not Taken.*

*Two roads diverged in a wood.*

It means that you are standing in front of two diverged paths. You don't know what the right way is, but you have to choose one of them in order to learn English correctly. You hope that there is no more waste in time and effort in learning English.

*And I took the one less traveled by.*

It means that many people study English grammar and memorize a lot of English vocabulary when they learn English. They also practice English reading a lot for English examinations. Some of them may have never thought about whether their way of studying is correct or not because people around them are studying in the same way. They cannot discover people around them who can listen to and speak English well. But they can definitely find people who can read and write English well. The wide route where many people are going indicates that people are only focusing on English grammar and reading examinations. They have never thought seriously about what real English ability is. They underestimate how important listening practice is and how valuable the dictation process is in the entire English learning process.

Miso Han: Maybe one of them is me! I have not cared about English listening.

Dr. Peter Lee: Don't be discouraged! From now on, you have to change the road from the old one to the new one. You have started to believe the fact that English listening practice is extremely important. Congratulations!

# 5

## Taking dictation is a must

Dr. Peter Lee: You also believe that taking dictation is a must in order to develop your English listening skills quickly. Based on your reaction, it shows me that you have finally taken the road which is less travelled among many English learners. You are worried about your decision. But do you know something?

Miso Han: About what?

Dr. Peter Lee: Are you aware that your old way of studying English, which you did for a long time, is definitely wrong, based on your own experience? I really guarantee that you will become a totally different person if you follow my English teaching method. It emphasizes that LISTENING and DICTATING are extremely important in learning English. Do you trust me?

Miso Han: I trust you.

Dr. Peter Lee: The last sentence of the poem *The Road Not Taken* is…

*...and that has made all the difference.*

Miso Han: What does it mean?

Dr. Peter Lee: It means that your decision has made you totally different. You will start to build the basis of learning English not from English grammar or a lot of English reading materials but from English LISTENING PRACTICE. You will start to listen to English every day using one English tape, which is not difficult for you. If you can understand about seventy percent of its content, you will choose it and listen to it continually. In that tape, there should not be any Korean explanation and translation. It is only recorded in English. You will listen to it every day for one hour, except Sunday. Some don't care for English listening practice. But you are different from other English learners because you realize what the right road for learning English is.

Miso Han: Now, I know the overall meaning of the poem. And I also understand that you used poetry in order for us to understand how important English listening is. Thank you so much! But what should I do after listening to one English tape over a hundred times? You said that the next step is taking dictation on it. However, you didn't let us know how to take dictation.

Dr. Peter Lee: I will explain to you now how to take dictation from an English tape, to which you have listened a hundred times. Taking dictation is similar to listening practice. As I mentioned earlier, you should listen to your chosen tape once or twice a day. In addition, you must avoid listening to it many times in just one day because that is not effective. You should also make sure that the amount of dictation fits only half a page to one page per day, not too many pages of dictation per day.

Remember that while taking dictation, you must not do too much of it in only one day. Some of you want to finish taking dictation in just a few days because you think that you know its content well. Don't do that! That is absolutely the wrong way of taking dictation on the English tape that you selected.

Miso Han: Why? Is there any particular reason?

Dr. Peter Lee: Yes, you must avoid taking dictation of the whole content in only one day. If you finish a specific amount of dictation today, then, you must read it aloud today. Don't postpone reading it for tomorrow! If you finished taking dictation of the whole content of an English tape in a day, it would be impossible for you to finish reading it aloud the same day. Some might say that they can read the whole content in a day. However, if you want to read it just like English native speakers, you must keep reading it for many months and not just for a day. That is why it would be good for you to take dictation of it in increments of about half a page or one page per day. After that activity, keep reading out loud what you wrote down on paper. You have to spend ten or fifteen minutes reading the dictated paper aloud. You also have to read it aloud every day except Sunday because, of course, you need to rest on Sundays.

Miso Han: How many times do I have to read each sentence?

Dr. Peter Lee: You have to read each sentence more than twenty times. You also have to consider intonation, accent, and rhyme spoken by English native speakers on the tape.

Miso Han: If I have to consider all the intonation, accent, and rhyme spoken by English native speakers on the tape, I need to read all the dictated sentences as many times as possible.

Dr. Peter Lee: Yes, you are right. Reading them aloud with the same intonation, accent, and rhyme spoken by English native speakers is the end of the English listening and speaking practice on the tape that you selected.

Miso Han: If I follow your recommendation, it will take several months to finish one English tape.

Dr. Peter Lee: Yes, you are right. Some of you may spend about three to six months or even a year to finish one English tape. Remember also that there is a connection within the process of listening- dictating-reading aloud.

Miso Han: I don't understand what you are saying. Would you please explain it more?

Dr. Peter Lee: Of course! Students choose English tapes to develop their listening skills. They also select English reading materials to enhance their reading skills. In addition, they choose English-speaking materials in order to increase their speaking skills. The problem is that all materials chosen are DIFFERENT from each other. There is no connection among them. If you want to quickly develop your English listening and speaking skill at the same time, you should select the one which helps your listening and speaking. One English tape!

Miso Han: Only one English tape?

Dr. Peter Lee: Yes, one English tape! Many students probably underestimate its potential power. However, the result of the completion of one English tape is not measurable because it is so effective.

Miso Han: Really? Only one English tape?

Dr. Peter Lee: Yes, you cannot imagine the power of only one English tape! You can also save hundreds of thousands of dollars otherwise spent on English programs abroad, if you know the power of using English tapes to learn the language.

Miso Han: Why?

Dr. Peter Lee: How much is one English tape?

Miso Han: I don't know exactly how much it is. It might cost about five dollars.

Dr. Peter Lee: How much money do you need to attend English programs abroad for a year? You probably need twenty to thirty thousand dollars. Why this much? It is because you have to pay ten to fifteen thousand dollars for tuition and fees per year. You also need to spend ten to fifteen thousand dollars for food, accommodation, transportation, and other extra expenses per year. Thus, if you want to attend English programs abroad for one year, you have to spend that amount of money. Of course, there are many benefits that you could gain from English programs abroad. But you could attain a lot of those benefits just as well from finishing only one English tape.

Miso Han: So do you think that attending English programs abroad is not useful? I think that staying in English countries is a good way to learn not only English but also culture.

Dr. Peter Lee: I am not talking about culture here. I have also never said that participating in English programs abroad is bad. I am talking about the quality and quantity of learning professional knowledge in English.

I don't have any right to say that attending English programs abroad is right or wrong. I am telling you about the effectiveness of both participating in English programs abroad and completing one English tape in learning English. I know it is hard to compare. However, I would like to emphasize the effectiveness of completing one English tape with minimal cost. Many students simply imagine that if they studied abroad in English programs for one year, they could use English without difficulty. Some of them are successful while others are not. This is a reality of life.

Seongsil Park: It depends on whether they study hard.

Dr. Peter Lee: You are right! However, some of those students who spent a year in English programs abroad also need to develop their listening skills. In English programs abroad, they may have many chances to listen to what English native speakers say and chances to talk to them in English. However, most realize that there are not many differences between learning in English programs abroad and learning in Korea. They also think that there are actually not many chances to talk in English with native speakers. They realize that the effectiveness of learning English in English programs abroad is similar to that offered in Korea.

Seongsil Park: Really?

Dr. Peter Lee: Yes, they have finally become aware of the fact that considering all the circumstances and the English native speakers around them, all these are not significant in influencing their personal English ability. The most important thing in learning English is their mindset. They should believe that they can OVERCOME any obstacles which interfere with their English learning process. At last they realize that they don't need a perfect place or a lot of money for learning English.

Seongsil Park: Then, what do they need?

Dr. Peter Lee: They only need one English tape! They just have to listen to it every day except on Sunday. When they completely finish listening to it, taking diction of it, and reading it aloud, their English listening and speaking skills will have dramatically improved. In addition, their intonation and accent would by then be quite similar to that of English native speakers. Through English listening and speaking practice with only one English tape, their intonation and accent will be effectively and efficiently trained. There is one more thing that you have to know.

Seongsil Park: What is that?

Dr. Peter Lee: You can also generate a lot of sentences by remixing the sentences found in the English tape to which you listened. Let me show you how it works.

For example, there are two sentences on the English tape. One is *'I am sitting on a chair'* and the other is *'reading a newspaper'*. If I combine these two sentences to make one, it can be the following sentence.

*'I am sitting on a chair while reading a newspaper.'*

This is a new sentence created by mixing two sentences.

Miso Han: Oh, I see. But from how many tapes do I have to take dictation? And until when do I have to take dictation?

Dr. Peter Lee: There are several steps in each level of dictation. There are also three main categories of taking dictation, including English tape dictation, English movie dictation, and English news dictation.

Miso Han: Which one is the first, second, and third?

Dr. Peter Lee: There is no specific order among them. However, I would like to recommend for you to take dictation from English tapes because it is easier to replay and fast-forward an English tape than to traverse movies and news. You just need a cassette player to listen to a cassette tape. In general, cassette tapes are recorded clearly because they are made for listening, not for watching, so that you can concentrate on listening to it.

Miso Han: In that case, I am going to listen to English tapes wherever I go and whatever I do.

Dr. Peter Lee: That is fine, but you must remember one thing while listening to an English tape.

Miso Han: What is that?

Dr. Peter Lee: You must concentrate on listening to it at least once a day. As I mentioned earlier, you have to spend thirty minutes listening to an English tape. During that time, you must focus on listening to it without doing anything else. You must be concentrated fully while listening to it. You said that you are going to listen to it wherever you go. On the way home or to school, you are distracted by buildings and people passing by, so that it could be hard for you to focus on listening to it. There may be a lot of distractions that take your focus away from listening to it. Thus, you need to concentrate fully while listening to the tape. I used to just sit on a chair and listen, in order to maximize my concentration. You must remember that English listening practice is one of the most important parts of learning English.

Miso Han: I didn't know about that. I just thought that there would be no particular requirements for listening to English tapes.

Dr. Peter Lee: If you studied English without any particular strategy in the past, please don't do it anymore. From now on, you have to think about specific strategies for how to study and learn English. You should also think about how to use your time and effort effectively for learning English.

Miso Han: Oh, I see. I don't want to make the same mistakes any more in learning English. Then, what should I do?

Dr. Peter Lee: As I said, you must focus on listening to an English tape for thirty minutes. Do you know where the best place is?

Miso Han: I don't know.

Dr. Peter Lee: You can find a good place around you for English listening practice. What about your room at home? It is one of the best places to focus on listening to English tapes.

Miso Han: What if I don't have my own room at home?

Dr. Peter Lee: What about a public library or university library? You just need a cassette player and an English tape. Oh, I am sorry. You also need a headset or earphones.

Miso Han: Right. You are right. But where could I practice reading dictation aloud?

Dr. Peter Lee: That is such a great question! Now you know how to discuss. You are asking me many questions in order to figure out the problems related to English education.

Actually, when I was young, your question was one of the most serious concerns in my life because I also needed that kind of place. I wanted to listen to English tapes with full concentration and without distractions. In addition, I wanted to take dictation of English tapes which I had listened to more than a hundred times. I wanted to practice reading the dictated papers aloud every day as well, except Sunday, of course. However, you know what? I felt it was difficult for me to do it.

Miso Han: Why? Was there someone who interrupted your English learning activities?

Dr. Peter Lee: No.

Miso Han: Did you have to work hard to cover your university tuition and fees so that you did not have enough time to study?

Dr. Peter Lee: No.

Miso Han: Then, why?

Dr. Peter Lee: It is because there were not many good places for me to listen to the tapes without distractions. Actually, I listened to English tapes in my room for one or two hours a day. However, I could not focus on them after one and a half months. Do you know how hard it is to focus on listening to an English tape one hour a day? However, I wanted a place where many students could practice their English listening and speaking skills.

Miso Han: Where? Did you find it?

Dr. Peter Lee: I found a place like that, which is called an English laboratory. Twenty years ago, English laboratories were found in many universities and public libraries. In an English laboratory, there were tape recorders so that students listened to English tapes, took dictations of them, and finally read dictated papers aloud. Even if their voices were very loud, there was nobody interrupting their English speaking practice.

Miso Han: Really? But nowadays, when I want to use an English laboratory at a public library, I have to be quiet there because many people are watching movies using headsets, without speaking practice. If I speak English loudly there, they might hit me or be angry at me.

Dr. Peter Lee: You are right. Nowadays, an English laboratory is not a place for listening to English and speaking English, but only a place for watching movies in order to relax. This is totally the opposite way of helping English learners. I don't know who decided to install a lot of cutting-edge equipment in English libraries for watching movies in order to relax. Students can relax at home! An English laboratory is NOT a theater, but a place for listening to English and speaking English.

Miso Han: I have never seen students practicing their English speaking in an English laboratory. I think that there are other places to practice English reading and speaking. They probably want to watch English movies, listen to English tapes, or take dictations in an English laboratory. After doing these activities, they go home and read dictated papers aloud. What about this way?

Dr. Peter Lee: You may be right but you may also be wrong. If students used English laboratories in order to listen to English tapes, watch English movies, or take dictation, that would be fine. If they read dictated papers aloud at home, that would also be great. However, can you do it every day at home? What if you have to do all these English learning activities for three or four years? Can you go through all these processes alone?

Miso Han: Maybe not.

Dr. Peter Lee: Why not?

Miso Han: Because I don't want to do it alone. I would probably feel lonely.

Dr. Peter Lee: You are right. You feel alone and you need somebody. Why do you want to go to a library? Studying together would probably be more effective than studying alone. You could focus on studying even if there is no one you know in the library. I am talking, of course, about the atmosphere of a public library. A library is a place for studying academic subjects, reading books, watching movies, and so on. There are various services offered in a library. People go to a library because they think that doing something in a library is more productive than doing it alone at home. Do you agree with this?

Miso Han: Yes, I do agree.

Dr. Peter Lee: What if you are going to an English laboratory not only to listen to English tapes, to watch English movies, and to take dictation but also to read English materials aloud because they allow you to do it. You don't worry about your voice. In an English laboratory there is nobody covering your mouth because your voice is too loud while reading. The atmosphere is not absolutely strange because all of the students in an English laboratory are reading English materials aloud. They are creating the right atmosphere for an English laboratory.

Miso Han: Oh, it would be wonderful! If there were that kind of place, I would go there to practice English speaking during weekdays.

Dr. Peter Lee: Yes, that would be great. When you attend English classes, you usually listen to what teachers are saying in English.

Miso Han: You are right. I don't have enough opportunity to talk in English.

Dr. Peter Lee: What if you go to an English laboratory to practice English speaking for an hour every day before going home? You could become a good English speaker after some time. I am sure of that. Of course, you have to spend at least two or three years doing this.

Miso Han: I will do it. I will do it. I am a freshman and if I do this regularly for four years until graduation, I could become a good English speaker.

Dr. Peter Lee: I know you can do it! I definitely believe that you can achieve your goal. That is why we are going to open the JC English laboratory at school next week. Don't expect too much though. It is very lightly equipped. There are only twelve desks and chairs, including headsets and tape recorders. There is also a chalkboard. I will show you its design.

Miso Han: Did you design this?

Dr. Peter Lee: Yes, I did. What do you think? Is it good?

Miso Han: There is only one computer. Why did you put in only one computer?

Dr. Peter Lee: The computer desk is for an assistant who is assigned to check how many students come to practice English listening and speaking. If you turn your chair, you can see each other in order to discuss some topics in English.

Miso Han: That is why there is a chalkboard.

Dr. Peter Lee: You are right. You are very astute.

Miso Han: Oh, thank you for the compliment!

Dr. Peter Lee: This is my whole picture of the English laboratory that I designed. Twelve students come to the English laboratory at eight o'clock in the morning. They listen to an English tape for thirty minutes. If they plan to listen to it more than a hundred times, they have to listen to it twice a day for fifty days. After listening to it completely more than a hundred times, they will start to take dictation of it for fifteen minutes per day.

Miso Han: So if I have finished listening to the selected English tape more than a hundred times, I don't need to listen to it any more. Is that right?

Dr. Peter Lee: Yes, you are right. After you have finished listening to the first English tape, then you will start the second English tape. You will also need to listen to the second English tape for thirty minutes a day, except Sunday. I will explain this later. But are you wondering about what you have to do for the rest of the fifteen minutes?

Miso Han: Read dictation aloud!

Dr. Peter Lee: Thank you, Miso. You are right! You have to read your dictated paper aloud for fifteen minutes. What I just said is the complete process of spending an hour doing the English listening, dictating, and speaking practices. What do you think?

Miso Han: Maybe it will work!

Dr. Peter Lee: No, it will DEFINITELY work! If you follow my instruction and spend an hour during the semester in the English laboratory at school for four years, you can definitely become a good English speaker. There is no doubt in my mind that will happen!

Miso Han: Your teaching seems reliable and trustworthy.

Dr. Peter Lee: You still don't believe my teaching.

Miso Han: No, I trust you. But the problem is that I do know who I am. I am not patient. I probably could not do it on my own.

Dr. Peter Lee: That is why you need a mentor. In addition, you need fellow students or friends who can practice English listening, dictating, and speaking in the English laboratory. You also need to know one more thing.

Miso Han: What is that?

Dr. Peter Lee: Confidence!

Miso Han: Confidence?

Dr. Peter Lee: Yes, confidence. Have you ever been confident about the English learning methods that you followed?

Miso Han: No, I am still not confident about my method of learning English. However, I trust your method.

Dr. Peter Lee: If you trust it, then you should follow me. However, I cannot force you to follow my instructions. It is up to you to decide whether you would like follow my method or not. But I will tell you one more thing. Do you know why you have uncertainty in your mind about my method? Because you have not experienced it before and you don't know exactly whether my method is right or wrong?

Miso Han: Yes, you are right.

Dr. Peter Lee: However, what if you try to spend your time on my instructions for only three months?

Miso Han: Only three months?

Dr. Peter Lee: I am not talking about whether you could finish learning English within three months. Do you think that it would be possible? Some advertisements show that you could be a master of English after just three to six months if you use some particular English materials. Do you believe this?

Gamsa Yang: I cannot believe it.

Dr. Peter Lee: Yes, you are right. I really want to meet the authors of the book who claim that English learners can satisfactorily learn English within three to six months if they use their books. I really would like to say that it would be impossible to finish learning English within one or five or even ten years. You have to keep learning English and learning never ends. Honestly, that is the truth.

Gamsa Yang: Really? That is such a long period of time! I couldn't do it for that long.

Dr. Peter Lee: Don't worry. I don't expect you to study English for your whole life. There are many other exciting subjects. English is a language which is one of the more effective communication tools used in international business. It can help you broaden your horizons and job opportunities as well. It will also help you accomplish your ultimate dream.

Gamsa Yang: I really hope to use English well.

Dr. Peter Lee: That day will come if you have confidence. I really like the following sentences written in the Bible.

*Therefore don't cast away your confidence, which has great reward. For you have need of endurance, so that after you have done the will of God, you may receive the promise (Hebrews 10: 35-36).*

Gamsa Yang: Confidence, endurance, and promise? What are these?

Dr. Peter Lee: If you know how to learn English, you may be confident. However, you don't know exactly how to learn English. Even if you have studied English hard for more than ten years, from elementary school to high school, you hesitate to speak English in front of foreigners. Why do you think this is so?

Gamsa Yang: I have no idea at all. Can you explain it to us?

Dr. Peter Lee: Of course. I would be glad to explain it to you. You hesitate to talk in front of foreigners because you don't have confidence to do so. I am sure your next question is, "What is confidence?" Well, confidence is a kind of personal belief and faith in yourself that you can achieve your goal. It also means that you know the right direction in order to achieve your goal. As time goes by, you will be much closer to the goal than before because you know the right direction. You will be confident because you make an effort to achieve your goal. You will also make progress in developing your ability because you know the right path to achieving your goal. In the case of learning English, I believe that it is the same thing! Are you confident about learning English using your own method? Can you keep following the English learning methods of other people for the next ten years? I would like to ask a question one more time. Do you have confidence about your own English learning method?

Gamsa Yang: No, I am not confident at all. Actually, I want to give up learning English. I don't want to waste any more time. I could spend the time that I have wasted on learning English in other productive ways. How could I be confident about learning English? Sometimes, I think that I am not eligible to learn English. I mean that I don't have a talent for English.

Dr. Peter Lee: Oh, don't give up learning English and don't be frustrated. Don't say that you don't have a talent for English. You must not underestimate your potential and your talent. There is no problem in you. But there are a lot of problems in your English learning method. If you say that you cannot do it, then nobody can do it for you. You have to remember that your tongue has the power of life and death. If you remind yourself that you can do it, then you really CAN do it. If there are some obstacles and barriers along the way, try to overcome them. I want to tell you a story.

Gamsa Yang: What is that?

Dr. Peter Lee: If you watch programs in which people overcome hardships in their life, you may be encouraged. What if your classmates are successful in learning English by following my instruction? I really expect you to follow my instruction for this semester. Take up the challenge! I will help you.

Gamsa Yang: I will follow your instructions. On the basis of your teaching, I will choose one English tape in which I can understand about seventy percent of the content. After selecting an English tape recorded only in English, I will listen to it daily for thirty minutes during weekdays, except Sunday. When I have finished listening to it more than a hundred times, I will start to take dictation of it for fifteen minutes. You also said that if I finished listening to the first tape for a hundred times, I don't need to listen to it any more. After finishing the first tape, I have to listen to the second English tape following the method that I did in the previous listening practice. Is that right?

Dr. Peter Lee: Yes, you are right. What is the next step?

Gamsa Yang: After taking dictation of it, I will read aloud the dictated paper for fifteen minutes.

Dr. Peter Lee: Yes, you are exactly right. You are very smart! There is nothing missing of the main ideas. You mentioned them all, actually.

Gamsa Yang: Thank you so much!

Dr. Peter Lee: Can you do the whole process for three months?

Gamsa Yang: Yes, I will.

Dr. Peter Lee: Don't give it up! You have to think that it is a very good chance to develop your English ability. You are a freshman. If you do this process for four years, you will be a very good English speaker when you graduate. You will also get a good job after graduation because of your English ability. I am sure that you will be very confident in listening and speaking English in the future.

Gamsa Yang: Really? But wait, why will I get a good job if I speak good English?

Dr. Peter Lee: Of course. If you persevere, you will greatly improve your English abilities. You won't give up learning English even if someone interrupts your English learning. You won't stop doing this English learning process when you recognize that this method really works. You can identify whether it works or not by your own learning experience. And then you will be very confident in learning English.

Gamsa Yang: Now I understand how I can be confident. Thank you so much for sharing with us your English learning method. Wait, you have not answered my questions on getting a good job if I speak good English.

Dr. Peter Lee: You are welcome. This is my job. Now, in relation to your question on how you can get a good job if you speak good English, it is a given fact that employers prefer personnel who are fluent in the English language because English happens to be the universal language used for business. I hope this clarifies your query.

# 6

## The English ground in the brain

Dr. Peter Lee: Now, are you wondering what the next step is?

Gamsa Yang: Is there a next step?

Dr. Peter Lee: Sure. I will tell you another secret!

Gamsa Yang: What is that?

Dr. Peter Lee: The next step is about how to absorb English vocabulary.

Gamsa Yang: Is it possible to absorb English vocabulary? English vocabulary is not a liquid which can be soaked up.

Dr. Peter Lee: Oh, that is what I mean to say. In general, students think that memorizing English vocabulary is one hard task that they have to do in learning English. An English word is a basic element like a brick to build your English building. The method by which to learn English vocabulary should be a basic concern in establishing your English competency.

Gamsa Yang: Is there any particular method for learning English vocabulary? I just think that memorizing is one of the best ways of learning English vocabulary.

Dr. Peter Lee: Just memorize? Do you think that is correct advice for learning English?

Gamsa Yang: On the basis of your instruction, it would be an incorrect answer.

Dr. Peter Lee: You are right! Rote memorization is an incorrect answer. Of course, it is not a hundred percent incorrect.

Gamsa Yang: Would you explain why rote memorization was an incorrect answer, even though you said that it was not a hundred percent incorrect?

Dr. Peter Lee: I always emphasize the right steps of learning English. In the four English learning competencies of listening, speaking, reading, and writing, one must always take listening practice first. I have already explained it in the first section of this class.

Gamsa Yang: Yes, you explained how important English listening practice was.

Dr. Peter Lee: Alright. Then, you have to listen carefully to what I am going to say from now on. This is a very important secret of learning English that many people don't know.

Gamsa Yang: What is that?

Dr. Peter Lee: English listening practice is the best and most unique way to form the English ground in your brain.

Gamsa Yang: The English ground in my brain?

Dr. Peter Lee: Yes, you can make your own English ground in

your brain by engaging actively in English listening practice. I have never investigated scientifically whether there is an English ground in my brain or not after doing English listening practice. However, I will refer to the capacity of your brain which is created by English listening practice as "English ground."

Gamsa Yang: The English ground in my brain?

Dr. Peter Lee: Yes, the English ground in your brain. I will explain it in detail.

In general, students start to learn English from elementary or middle school. They normally learn English grammar, reading, and vocabulary rather than listening. Please raise your hand if you started learning English from listening practice.

Students in the class: (No one raises his/her hand.)

Dr. Peter Lee: See? Nobody learned English from listening practice. That is the biggest problem in your English learning process. When you were young, you were probably tested at school on whether you knew English grammar and vocabulary. If you had bad scores on English examinations at school, you would have thought that you were not good at English grammar. You would also have thought that you needed to memorize a lot of English vocabulary. However, you would never have thought about what the real problem was in your English learning process. In reality, you just focused on English grammar, reading, and vocabulary.

Gamsa Yang: Yes, you are right. I am amazed that you know

exactly what I did.

Dr. Peter Lee: I can also guess how you and other students used to memorize English vocabulary. There are many episodes related to how Korean students memorize English vocabulary. For example, students buy an English dictionary in order to memorize the all of English vocabulary. They plan to memorize one page of the English dictionary every day. It is hard for them to memorize all the words on a page of the English dictionary. However, they do it continuously, believing that memorizing the whole English dictionary would do them good! Do you think that it is possible for you to memorize all the English vocabulary written in the English dictionary?

Gamsa Yang: Maybe it's possible.

Dr. Peter Lee: Yes, you are right. However, I hope you find more efficient ways of learning English vocabulary. You have never memorized Korean vocabulary using the Korean dictionary in order to learn Korean. Is that right? You should always remember the truth that learning foreign languages is always the same or similar to learning your mother tongue. Please remember this always!

Gamsa Yang: Yes, I will.

Dr. Peter Lee: Alright. Then, I will explain the importance of English listening practice in learning English vocabulary. Can you guess the number of English words? There are hundreds of thousands of English words. It would be impossible for you to memorize all of them. Let us look at the Korean dictionary. There are also hundreds of thousands of Korean words in it. There is no Korean who decides to memorize all of the vocabulary written in the Korean dictionary. There is also no Korean who forces himself to memorize all the words written in the Korean dictionary while learning Korean. Have you ever pushed yourself to memorize Korean vocabulary while learning Korean?

Gamsa Yang: No.

Dr. Peter Lee: Then, why have you pushed yourself to memorize English vocabulary?

Gamsa Yang: Because English is not my mother tongue.

Dr. Peter Lee: I know that English is not your mother tongue. However, you have to remember that the way of learning English is the same or similar to learning Korean. I am not saying that your effort to memorize English vocabulary is wrong. However, I really want you to know the most efficient way of learning English vocabulary.

Gamsa Yang: So what should I do? Is there some important process that I have to know in order to learn English vocabulary?

Dr. Peter Lee: Yes, there is something that you must know.

PERFORM ENGLISH LISTENING PRACTICE!

Gamsa Yang: Again? Do you think that English listening practice significantly influences the process of learning English vocabulary?

Dr. Peter Lee: Yes, I absolutely, totally, definitely, and completely believe it. If you do English listening practice when you are beginning to learn English, you can memorize English vocabulary much more easily than someone who has never done English listening practice. Actually, in this case, I don't want to use the word *memorize*. I want to use the word *absorb* instead because the word absorb is more proper than *memorize* in this case. English listening practice allows you to *absorb* English vocabulary into your brain. This is definitely true, even though I cannot prove it scientifically.

Gamsa Yang: I cannot believe it. Is it possible for someone whose mother tongue is not English to absorb or be proficient in English vocabulary?

Dr. Peter Lee: Yes, it is possible. However, you need time and effort. You need to set aside a specific time to listen to English during the week and listen to it repeatedly. If you keep listening to English, you can form your English ground in your brain and, in the process, it will help you to absorb English vocabulary.

Gamsa Yang: Really?

Dr. Peter Lee: Yes, it is true! Maybe you have experienced this process when you learned Korean. You didn't need to memorize Korean vocabulary when you learned Korean. The reason is that you listened to Korean since you were born. Your father and mother always talk to you in Korean. After you listened to the Korean language from your parents or other people around you for several years, you finally opened your mouth to say one or two words in Korean. This is the beginning of the process for how every human being learns his/her mother tongue. Do you think it is wrong?

Gamsa Yang: No, it is definitely right. But I still don't understand the concept of 'absorbing English vocabulary.'

Dr. Peter Lee: I know. But it is definitely true. Doing English listening practice is the most effective way of absorbing English vocabulary.

Gamsa Yang: Thus, you expect me to do English listening practice in order to memorize English vocabulary easily. Is that right?

Dr. Peter Lee: Yes, you are right. Don't you believe it? Then, why don't you take a test that I suggest? Do you know the word *relinquish*?

Gamsa Yang: No, I don't know.

Dr. Peter Lee: Its meaning is give up. I will introduce an example of the way for absorbing English vocabulary. Please listen to the word and follow me in reading aloud.

Gamsa Yang: Yes, I will.

Dr. Peter Lee: Relinquish!

Students in the class: Relinquish!

Dr. Peter Lee: Relinquish!

Students in the class: Relinquish!

Dr. Peter Lee: Relinquish means give up.

Students in the class: Relinquish means give up.

Dr. Peter Lee: Yes, that is it. It is simple to follow. You can remember its meaning, right?

Gamsa Yang: Right. The meaning of relinquish is to give up.

Dr. Peter Lee: Yes, you are right. You don't need to write it down in your notes in order to memorize it. Usually you kept your mouth closed, so that you didn't pronounce it. That is not the right way of learning English vocabulary. You have to open your mouth to pronounce it. If you pronounce it, your ears will hear it. Then, your mental faculties will save it in your brain. Research indicates that your brain can remember the information very well when it is spoken out loud. That is why you have to say it in order to absorb English vocabulary. Thus, this means that you don't use your hands to write down the words in a notebook. Do you understand?

Gamsa Yang: Yes, I understand.

Dr. Peter Lee: You kept pronouncing it with me and I told you about its meaning. Through this whole process of repetition, its sound, meaning, and letters are automatically absorbed in your brain. How is it possible?

Seongsil Park: I think that we listened to its pronunciation spoken by you and we followed to read it aloud. You also explained its meaning and we listened to it. You kept reading the word aloud and we listened to it and followed your pronunciation. That is all.

Dr. Peter Lee: That is right.

Seongsil Park: In the past, I used my hand to write down English words several times in order to memorize them. I didn't listen to it and read it aloud as well. Without using my mouth and ears, I tried to memorize English vocabulary.

Dr. Peter Lee: That is a big mistake.

Seongsil Park: Yes, now I know.

Dr. Peter Lee: Have you studied English without pronouncing it?

Seongsil Park: Yes, I have because I have usually studied English in a library. As you know, I must be quiet in a library.

Dr. Peter Lee: Have you ever checked correct English pronunciations?

Seongsil Park: No, I haven't.

Dr. Peter Lee: Your problem is more serious than I thought. Do you think that your method of memorizing English vocabulary is right?

Seongsil Park: No, it's not.

Dr. Peter Lee: Then, why didn't you change it?

Seongsil Park: First of all, I don't know the right way of memorizing English vocabulary. Second of all, many students around me do the same thing, thus I simply imitate them.

Dr. Peter Lee: You have just followed other students around you without knowing whether it was right or wrong?

Seongsil Park: Yes, I have.

Dr. Peter Lee: Are you going to keep following those incorrect methods?

Seongsil Park: No, I don't want to follow them anymore because they are useless. I cannot trust my method anymore. I have finally realized that my method is absolutely wrong, as proven by my own experience. If my English learning method worked well, I would speak English well.

Dr. Peter Lee: You are right. Then, please read the following sentence aloud.

*I relinquish the old method of memorizing English vocabulary because it is not worthy. I want to start a new method of learning English vocabulary.*

Students in the class: *I relinquish the old method of memorizing English vocabulary because it is not worthy. I want to start a new method of learning English vocabulary.*

# 7

## The English-Korean and English-English dictionary

Dr. Peter Lee: Alright. Then, I will let you know about another important way of learning English vocabulary. It is about both the English-English dictionary and the English-Korean dictionary. I really recommend that you use both of them.

Seongsil Park: Do I always have to use both of them?

Dr. Peter Lee: Not always, but in general you need to use both of them.

Seongsil Park: Why?

Dr. Peter Lee: That is a good question. There are many reasons why you have to use both of them. The most important reason is that it could help you understand the overall meaning of English vocabulary. Many Korean students make an English vocabulary note. They write down English words and read them wherever they go. Have you ever made that kind of an English vocabulary note?

Seongsil Park: Yes, I have.

Dr. Peter Lee: Is it working well for helping you remember English vocabulary? Would you tell me about your English vocabulary note, please?

Seongsil Park: It was very easy to make it. I prepared a note and a pen. When I found English words that I didn't know, I wrote them down on my note. I divided my note into two parts. And I wrote down English words on the left side and their Korean meanings on the right side.

Dr. Peter Lee: And then what did you do?

Seongsil Park: I covered the Korean part with my hand and then tried to remember Korean meanings. That was all about my English vocabulary notes.

Dr. Peter Lee: Did you add example sentences for helping you remember the meanings of English vocabulary?

Seongsil Park: I did. But I gave it up when I felt that it didn't work well. It was too boring and hard. After writing down more than three hundred English words in my English notes, I had difficulty reviewing all of them. I couldn't remember all the English words that I noted down, especially when the number of English vocabulary reached over five hundred. I could remember approximately thirty or forty percent of the English words in it. I have tried to make these English notes several times, but I gave it up because I was not confident of success in this whole process of learning English vocabulary.

Dr. Peter Lee: Learning many English words is not easy. If you want to use English well, you have to overcome the process of learning English vocabulary. If you don't know many English words, then you cannot listen to and speak English well. Some might say that you can use English well if you know only three to five hundred English words. It might be right sometimes, but it could also be wrong. However, you will need to know more English vocabulary if you don't understand English programs, English newspapers, and so on. You will feel more confident if you know a lot of English words.

Seongsil Park: You are right. However, I feel some difficulty when I keep on memorizing and reviewing a lot of English words.

Dr. Peter Lee: That is why you need a strategy to help you memorize and review English vocabulary.

Seongsil Park: Do you have a specific strategy for that?

Dr. Peter Lee: Yes, I do! In order to let you know the right method of learning English vocabulary, you need to understand the following sentence. You can discover the answer about your question in this sentence.

Here it goes:

*But he who received seed on the good ground is he who hears the word and understands it, who indeed bears fruit and produces: some a hundredfold, some sixty, some thirty (Matthew 13:23)*

Seongsil Park: I still don't know the answer.

Dr. Peter Lee: Look at the sentence carefully. There is a clue for you to figure out the answer. Please find important words in it.

Seongsil Park: Maybe, the *good ground*?

Dr. Peter Lee: Exactly correct. You are genius! I will explain it in detail.

First, you have to make good English ground in your brain in order to absorb English vocabulary. I mentioned repeatedly that you have to do listening practice in order to learn English because it is the basic step in learning a language. Is that right?

Seongsil Park: Right.

Dr. Peter Lee: When you listen to English from radio or watch English programs on television, it is a good way to make the English ground in your brain. If you have listened to English for a long time, a good English ground in your brain has already been made. If you don't understand it, I will give you an example.

For example, you have listened to the Korean language since you were born, and that means that you have had a good Korean ground in your brain. That is why you don't need to memorize Korean vocabulary. It is automatically absorbed in your brain through time. That is the evidence that you have a good Korean ground in your brain.

Seongsil Park: You are right! I have never tried to memorize Korean vocabulary. I also didn't need to review Korean vocabulary. When I didn't know Korean vocabulary, then I would ask my parents its meaning. They explained it and I understood. When they explained the Korean vocabulary several times, I never forget its meaning, even after several years.

Dr. Peter Lee: You are genius!

Seongsil Park: Why?

Dr. Peter Lee: Because you didn't forget the meaning of Korean vocabulary after listening to its explanation.

Seongsil Park: No, I asked it several times when I didn't understand its meaning. However, I am sure that I don't need any review of Korean vocabulary because it is absorbed automatically in my brain.

Dr. Peter Lee: That is what I am talking about. You didn't have to memorize or review Korean vocabulary at all while learning it. This is because you already have a good Korean ground of absorbing it by frequently hearing and listening to the Korean language since you were born.

Seongsil Park: What is the difference between hearing and listening?

Dr. Peter Lee: Hearing is the process of being aware of a sound but listening is the process of paying attention to it and focusing on the message. When you were born, you didn't listen to what your parents said. You just heard their words.

Seongsil Park: I see what you mean. So a good English ground in my brain is also important for learning English vocabulary. I regret I never knew this before.

Dr. Peter Lee: Why?

Seongsil Park: Because if I had listened to English since I was very young, I would have had a good English ground in my brain. As a result, I could absorb all of the English information that I hear and listen to in my English ground without too much effort. I have spent too many hours memorizing English vocabulary. If I had known the importance of English listening practice, I would have spent many hours listening to English when I was young.

Dr. Peter Lee: Don't regret it. You are still young. You have plenty of time to do English listening practice.

Seongsil Park: Yes, you are right! You really dislike negative words, right? You like positive words like the following sentence.

WE STILL HAVE A CHANCE!

Dr. Peter Lee: You are definitely right. If you believe that you can achieve your goal, then you can accomplish it according to your faith. If you say that you cannot do it, there is nobody who can do it for you. If you believe that you want to use English well, you can use English well in the future. Of course, you must follow the right steps in learning English. Learning English is not difficult if you know the right steps. The first step to learn English is listening, as I always emphasize. The first step to learn English vocabulary, which is the basic element in establishing your English ability concretely, is LISTENING!

Gamdong Min: What is a good way of listening to English?

Dr. Peter Lee: There is no good way to listen to English. Do you have a computer or a smart phone?

Gamdong Min: Yes, I have both.

Dr. Peter Lee: Then, listen to the correct pronunciation of English vocabulary by using those two pieces of equipment. After checking the correct pronunciation, practice saying it over and over until your pronunciation is the same or similar to the sound that you listen to.

Gamdong Min: Is that all? I think many students know the method you recommend. That is not a special method or even a secret one.

Dr. Peter Lee: Oh, wait a minute! You have to be patient. Remember, I taught you that you have to use both the English-Korean dictionary and the English-English dictionary.

Gamdong Min: Yes, I remember.

Dr. Peter Lee: So it is time for you to learn how to use the English-English dictionary.

Gamdong Min: How do I use it?

Dr. Peter Lee: Many Korean students just write down the Korean meanings of English vocabulary without checking its English explanations from the English-English dictionary. If you check the meanings of English vocabulary using the English-English dictionary, there are not many explanations compared to

Korean meanings in the English-Korean dictionary. If you check the Korean meanings of the English word *essential*, you can find many explanations. Are there many students here who memorize many Korean meanings of English vocabulary?

Gamdong Min: I usually write down at least two or three Korean meanings of an English word in my English vocabulary notes.

Dr. Peter Lee: Why do you think that you have to know more than two or three Korean meanings of an English word? Knowing more than two or three Korean meanings of an English word is important because it will improve your vocabulary. One more important thing! Many Korean meanings of an English word are related to each other! Do you know why?

Gamdong Min: I don't know.

Dr. Peter Lee: Because one core meaning of an English word includes many related meanings. For example, the word *pretty* has many meanings such as the following: *good-looking, attractive, charming, beautiful*, and so on.

Gamdong Min: So how do I use the English-English dictionary?

Dr. Peter Lee: You must use an English-English dictionary properly. I will explain it using an example. I really like the word *dream*. Do you know the definition of the word *dream*?

Gamdong Min: Dream is something that I want to achieve.

Dr. Peter Lee: Yes, you are right. If you check the word *dream* using Webster's English Dictionary, it explains it is *'a series of thoughts, images,* or *emotions occurring during sleep', 'a visionary creation of the imagination',* or *'a strongly desired goal or purpose.'* If you check it using a Collins Cobuild English Dictionary, it explains, *'When you dream, you experience imaginary events in your mind while you are asleep'* or *'If you describe something as a particular person's dream, you think that it would be ideal for that person and that he or she would like it very much'* and other explanations.

Gamdong Min: It is quite complicated. If I know the meaning of the word *dream* using the English-Korean dictionary, that is enough. If I check it using the English-English dictionary, I have to try to understand its meanings through long explanations. It is difficult to understand.

Dr. Peter Lee: That is the point: it is what you must go through in order to learn English vocabulary. What is a sentence?

Gamdong Min: A sentence? A sentence is a combination of words.

Dr. Peter Lee: Yes, you are right. A sentence is comprised of multiple words revolving around one main idea. The right and clear way to understand a sentence is to comprehend the meanings of each word. The basic step to knowing English vocabulary is to check it using the English-English dictionary, even though it is difficult for you to understand the whole explanation. You really just have to try. As I said earlier, *"No pain, no gain."*

Gamdong Min: Is it an effective method for learning English words?

Dr. Peter Lee: Of course it is! It is an effective and precise way to learn English vocabulary. While you are reading all the English explanations, you can find other English words that you don't know in the sentence. If you don't know them, you have to check them because those words are basic words. Using those basic words, it is possible to explain every single English word. Do you know why?

Gamdong Min: I don't know.

Dr. Peter Lee: If a young boy asks you a word, how do you explain it or what kind of words will you use? Do you want to use difficult or easy words for helping a young boy to understand?

Gamdong Min: I will use simple words because a young boy may not have enough word knowledge.

Dr. Peter Lee: That is what I am talking about. If you check a word using the English-English dictionary, you can find simple explanations of each word. That is a way to help people understand English well. It would also be good for you to remember that the words that you don't know in sample sentences should be checked with the English-English dictionary.

Gamdong Min: I see. The basic words within the explanations and sample sentences in the dictionary should be known in order to understand and learn English vocabulary successfully.

Dr. Peter Lee: Yes, you are right. The explanations of English vocabulary written in the English-English dictionary are written with essential words that everyone should know. If you understand the meaning of an English word using the English-English dictionary, you can also learn how to use English correctly. That is very important!

Gamdong Min: Why?

Dr. Peter Lee: Have you ever heard of *Konglish*?

Gamdong Min: A *Konglish* expression is a way of using English in a Korean way.

Dr. Peter Lee: Why does it happen?

Gamdong Min: Because of an English-Korean dictionary?

Dr. Peter Lee: Yes, you are right. Using an English-Korean dictionary seriously influences how we use English. As I mentioned earlier, learning English vocabulary is the basic step in learning English. However, many Korean students, probably more than eighty percent, learn English vocabulary from the English-Korean dictionary. This is one of the opposite ways of learning English.

Gamdong Min: But if we learn English words using the English-English dictionary, it may be a time-consuming process. We cannot understand the English explanations of an English word because we don't know many English words.

Dr. Peter Lee: However, you have to use the English-English

dictionary. If necessary, it might be good for you to use an English-English dictionary made for kids. There are many pictures to help children understand. I don't mean that you have to go back to the basic steps that children do when they learn English vocabulary. However, you have to use the English-English dictionary in order to understand not only English explanations, but also English ways of speaking and writing in order to avoid learning *Konglish* expressions.

Gamdong Min: You also said that it would be good to use the English-Korean dictionary.

Dr. Peter Lee: Yes, I said that. But you need to use both the English-Korean and English-English dictionaries in order to help you better understand English vocabulary in a clear and precise manner.

Gamdong Min: Is there any other thing that I have to do for learning English vocabulary?

Dr. Peter Lee: You also need to write down English explanations on your English vocabulary notes.

Gamdong Min: You mean that we have to write down the whole explanation written in the English-English dictionary?

Dr. Peter Lee: No. You don't need to write down all of them in your English notes. I think that one or two explanations would be enough to write down in your English vocabulary notes. After writing down one or two English explanations, you need to read them aloud several times.

# 8

## Reading English materials aloud

Gamdong Min: Reading the summary of English vocabulary aloud is the same as reading the dictated paper of an English tape aloud. Is that right?

Dr. Peter Lee: Yes, that is right. If you read your dictated papers and English vocabulary notes aloud every day except Sunday, you can speak and write English very well. Learning English is very simple. If you want to listen to English well, you have to practice listening to English. If you want to speak English well, you have to practice speaking English. If you want to write English sentences well, you have to practice writing English sentences.

Gamdong Min: It seems very simple.

Dr. Peter Lee: My method is very simple and it is also scientifically right. Have you ever watched a scene describing how our ancestors during the Joseon dynasty learned a language?

THEY READ BOOKS ALOUD!

Seongsil Park: Yes, I have seen that kind of scene in many traditional dramas. Many language learners read books aloud when their teachers read them. I think that there were no cassette players and cassette tapes for teaching the right pronunciations then. I don't know if they had a dictionary during that time. But they thought that the best way to learn a language was following along verbally at the same time when their teacher was reading a book aloud.

Dr. Peter Lee: Yes, you are very smart. There is the key for how to learn a language. Have you ever seen our ancestors analyze any language grammar in a movie or drama? I have never seen it. They were just reading books aloud over and over. You know that our current language-learning environment is much better than that of the past. However, I cannot say that students educated using cutting-edge techniques or equipment for learning English in our modern society are better than our ancestors, who were simply reading books aloud after their teachers. The method that our ancestors did was a very simple method and there was no cutting-edge technique or equipment. However, they knew how to teach and learn a language correctly. The way to learn English is very simple, but I don't know why students are having difficulty learning it.

Seongsil Park: I think that reading English aloud is a good method for learning English. But I always have to consider

English grammar examinations. I personally find English grammar very difficult.

Dr. Peter Lee: I understand why you are having difficulty in learning English. I think you feel that you don't need to spend too much time studying English grammar. Do you want to become an English grammarian who examines the structure of English? Your wish is quite simple. You just want to listen to and speak English well. In addition, you just want to write English sentences correctly, right? I think that is your basic reason for learning English, right?

Seongsil Park: Yes, you are right.

Dr. Peter Lee: One more thing that I really want you to know is how to write English sentences well. I didn't explain it before. I recommended the English-English dictionary as well as the English-Korean dictionary. You need to use both of them. But if you want to increase your writing skill in English, you need to use the English-English dictionary.

Seongsil Park: Why?

Dr. Peter Lee: Because the English-English dictionary contains vocabulary in English and its explanations are also in English. Thus, your writing skill in English will improve. Do you know the best way to develop your writing skill in Korean?

Seongsil Park: I think that reading a lot of books is one of the best ways to develop my writing skill.

Dr. Peter Lee: Many students may have the same opinion. You

are right. But you need a strategy. You just said that reading a lot of books is a good way to enhance your writing skill. But many people are already reading books and there are few people who write sentences very well. Some universities give prospective students writing tests. Writing tests are designed to examine how you express your opinion clearly, logically, and concisely. One of the most successful ways to increase writing skill is to familiarize yourself with newspapers, especially the opinion section.

Seongsil Park: The opinion section?

Dr. Peter Lee: Yes, the EDITORIAL section, where the opinion section can be found, is actually the best model of good writing, with opinions that are stated clearly, logically, and concisely. But I am not going to tell you more about this. I am just telling you about how to increase your writing skill in English. The most important thing that you have to consider in English writing is the best model of English writing. Where are perfect sentences that you emulate? You need to find English sentences which are logically and grammatically correct so that you can similarly develop your writing skill in the correct manner.

Seongsil Park: Where can I find it?

Dr. Peter Lee: You can find hundreds of thousands of sentences in one book.

Seongsil Park: Where?

Dr. Peter Lee: The English-English dictionary! Have you ever asked a teacher who is an English native speaker to check your sentences?

Seongsil Park: Yes, I have. But I don't know why some English native teachers have different opinions about editing.

Dr. Peter Lee: That is not strange. You know that editors have different opinions about writing. There is no particular standard to judge that this editor is better than others. However, you have to remember one thing. When you are writing English sentences, your sentences should be clear and easily understood by the reader. I think that the best way to write a sentence is to make it clear and readable. Where can you find clear and readable sentences?

Seongsil Park: From the English-English dictionary.

Dr. Peter Lee: Yes, you are right. The function of the English-English dictionary is to help the reader understand the definitions as clearly and easily as possible. In addition, you can see in dictionaries many examples on how to use a word in various ways, helping you learn the right expression of English words you are interested in.

Seongsil Park: Now, I understand precisely why I have to use the English-English dictionary and how to use it correctly.

Dr. Peter Lee: So we have examined how to learn English from listening to writing. Do you understand the whole process of learning English from listening to writing?

Seongsil Park: Yes, but I think that I could understand better if you summarized again the whole process of learning English.

Dr. Peter Lee: Okay, did you know that the meaning of "education" is "repetition" in Hebrew. I am going to summarize all the process of learning English in the last section of this class. But before I do that, I would like to ask if you have any questions on what we have discussed so far?

Seongsil Park: Actually, I have a question. How many English tapes should I listen to and take dictation from?

Dr. Peter Lee: Oh, that is a good question.

Seongsil Park: I have another question. How many words do I have to write down with their explanations written in the English-English dictionary?

Dr. Peter Lee: Oh, that is also a good question. I will tell you the answers one by one.

First, there is no specific number of English tapes that you have to finish taking dictation from. However, I recommend five or six tapes for dictation.

Seongsil Park: Why five or six?

Dr. Peter Lee: There are several reasons. As I mentioned earlier, the meaning of education is related to repetition. You need to think about how to repeat the tapes that you have listened to. That is why I suggest five or six tapes. Let us talk about why five tapes are suggested for dictation.

I said that you have to select an English tape whose content, at least seventy percent of it, you can understand. When you are listening to it, you can understand the message well. However, it is possible that you are unfamiliar with some words in it, as spoken by English native speakers. You may ask, why? It is because their intonation and accent can get in the way of your understanding. In addition, the speed of the spoken English in a tape could be very fast. Thus, you have to listen to one English tape more than a hundred times.

After listening to an English tape more than a hundred times, you can handle all the sounds in it that are spoken by native English speakers. You can also foresee upcoming dialogues. Of course, you must remember that you should listen to one English tape with concentration. English listening practice must always be done with concentration.

Seongsil Park: I see. I must listen to English tapes with concentration.

Dr. Peter Lee: You probably need one and a half to two months to finish listening to the first English tape. If you are listening to the first English tape twice a day, except Sunday, you probably need eight or nine weeks. You might think that it will be quite boring to listen to with concentration. However, you must listen carefully to all the sounds in it.

After finishing the first tape, you have to start taking dictation of it. The amount of dictation is less than one page. After dictation, you should read it aloud for fifteen minutes. You should also consider the intonation, accent, rhyme, and speed that native English speakers would have, if they were the ones reading it. It is not easy for you to imitate their speaking. However, you should follow, as much as possible, their intonation, accent, and rhyme.

Seongsil Park: Could you tell me how many times I have to read aloud the sentences on which I took dictation?

Dr. Peter Lee: It depends on you. I used to read one sentence more than twenty times. However, the total amount of times that I read one sentence is about a hundred.

Seongsil Park: Did you say that I have to read each sentence a hundred times?

Dr. Peter Lee: There is a reason why I decided to read it a hundred times. It is definitely not because I like the number. However, I could remember a sentence well after reading it aloud more than a hundred times. When I spoke with someone in English, I could use some of the sentences that I practiced reading aloud. There are also two amazing facts that you can experience after reading the same sentence more than a hundred times. Of course, you can only have this experience after taking dictation from a tape you listened to more than a hundred times.

Seongsil Park: What is that?

Dr. Peter Lee: First, you can automatically memorize the sentence that you read aloud more than a hundred times. Many students just try to memorize an English sentence by reading it aloud more than a hundred times without really listening and doing the dictation process. You don't always need to make an effort to listen and take dictation if you want to memorize English sentences. However, the most effective way of memorizing English sentences is to listen to them many times and take dictation on them if you want. As I mentioned earlier, listening to an English tape, taking dictation of it, and reading the dictated paper aloud is the complete process of creating a good English ground in your brain.

While listening to an English tape, you may hear a word that you don't know. If you don't know the meaning of a word, you need to use both the English-English dictionary and the English-Korean dictionary. You also need to write down English sentences explained in the English-English dictionary and read these sentences aloud. You also need to check the correct pronunciation. This entire process for finishing the first English tape will take three to four months.

Seongsil Park: Will it take about three to four months to finish just one English tape?

Dr. Peter Lee: Why? Do you think that is too much time?

Seongsil Park: Yes, I think so. Is it worth spending three to four months to finish only one English tape?

Dr. Peter Lee: Yes, it is definitely worthwhile. I think that you are underestimating the power of one English tape. Earlier, I have already mentioned the potential power of finishing one English tape. Even if it takes three to four months to finish the first English tape, it will take less time to finish the second and the third English tape. Do you think that you need more time to finish listening to the following English tapes?

Seongsil Park: I don't know.

Dr. Peter Lee: This is a very important point that you should remember. The level of the first English tape is lower than the second one. You have to choose a second tape which has a higher level of English quality. Among the five English tapes that you choose, the first tape should be the easiest and the last the most difficult.

Seongsil Park: I see.

Dr. Peter Lee: I will tell you another important point. You may spend less time on the second English tape than the first one, even though the level of the second one is more difficult than the first one. Do you know why?

Seongsil Park: I don't know.

Dr. Peter Lee: The reason is, by the time that you finish the first English tape, your English ability will be better than it was before. You could not perceive the word *listen* while listening to the first English tape because you didn't know the sound L. Many students don't perceive and understand very simple English words such as *listen, like, light,* and other words that include an L sound. Do you know why?

Seongsil Park: I don't know.

Dr. Peter Lee: Even if they have seen those words from

English books many times, they have never LISTENED to their correct sound. Some of them have never learned the L sound before. However, if you perceive, learn, and understand the basic words from the first English tape, it will be easy for you to understand the second English tape. If you spend three months finishing the first English tape, I am certain that you will spend less than three months finishing the second English tape. As you keep taking dictation of the five English tapes, you realize that it takes less time to finish those English tapes, even if their levels are getting higher.

Seongsil Park: When is the end of dictation?

Dr. Peter Lee: When you finish taking dictation of the five English tapes, it is the end of the dictation process. If you have finished the five English tapes, then you can perceive *L, R, TH, V, F, WOULD, WILL,* and other confusing sounds correctly. Please remember that taking dictation on an English tape is not for understanding the meanings of English sentences. It is about whether or not you can listen to all the sounds spoken by English native speakers. After you have taken dictation of the five English tapes, it is time for you to repeat all of them.

Seongsil Park: Why five tapes? You didn't explain that yet.

Dr. Peter Lee: The reason is that five tapes can be reiterated once per week. As I said, you need to listen to one English tape twice a day for a week. If you finish taking dictation of five English tapes and you finish reading aloud what you wrote, you could read them repeatedly following the system described below:

You can plan to listen to the first tape twice on Monday. The second tape is for Tuesday, the third tape is for Wednesday, the fourth tape is for Thursday, and the last tape is for Friday. So you can repeat all the five tapes from Monday to Friday. If you want to finish six English tapes, then you will repeat the sixth English tape on Saturday. Do you understand now why five English tapes are proper and how to repeat them?

Seongsil Park: Yes, I understand. But I have a question. When do I have to start listening to the second English tape? In addition, you mentioned that one hour is appropriate to spend for learning English. But I think that I will have to spend more than an hour according to your instructions. If I started listening to the second tape, I would probably spend more than thirty minutes listening to it twice a day.

Dr. Peter Lee: That is a good question. I think that one hour is proper for you to spend every day on learning English. But if you are interested, you can spend two hours each day. I will give you another summary of your study plan.

According to my instructions, you are going to spend thirty minutes listening to the first English tape. But there is no dictation process when you just listen to the first English tape. Then, you need to listen to it twice a day so that you will spend an hour listening to the first English tape. If you start to take dictation of the first tape, please listen to the second tape only once. It will take about thirty minutes. Then, you will take dictation of the first English tape for fifteen minutes and read the dictated paper aloud for fifteen minutes. Thus, the total is an hour.

Seongsil Park: What if the length of an English tape is more than thirty minutes?

Dr. Peter Lee: If you select an English tape which is more than thirty minutes long, you need to listen to only one side of it. If you listen to only one side of it, you may spend twenty minutes on listening. But you actually decide how many minutes you shall devote to listening to the English tape.

When I was young, I used to listen to one English tape two or three hours per day. I sat on a chair, focusing on listening to it. I used to go to the English laboratory of a public library. I had to be quiet there so I just listened with concentration to English tapes for two or three hours. The laboratory had big windows on the wall so that library users could see inside. I sat down on a chair, put my hands on a desk, and made my back straight in order to focus on listening to it. Sometimes, I closed my eyes to focus on listening to it. I had to remind myself that I had to focus on listening to it. But I realized that it would be better for me to listen to it looking at the wall instead of closing my eyes. When I closed my eyes, I got more distracted, so I usually looked at the wall while listening to it. Actually it is a secret that I marked a dot on the wall and looked straight at it in order to focus on listening to the tape. Please don't tell anyone about this.

Seongsil Park: I think that you tried many methods to study English.

Dr. Peter Lee: Of course. I believe that there is a shortcut to learning English. I will tell you about my personal story later. But I will tell you now about how to manage your time for learning English daily, even though I have already mentioned it. When you listen to the first English tape, you will listen to it twice a day because there is no dictation process. After listening to the tape more than a hundred times, you will start taking dictation of it.

Seongsil Park: Yes, I know this.

Dr. Peter Lee: When you start to take dictation of the first English tape, you need to spend fifteen minutes on it. After taking dictation for fifteen minutes, you will have to read the dictated paper aloud for fifteen minutes. If you want to check English vocabulary using the English-English dictionary or the English-Korean dictionary, remember that you need to spend more time for learning English daily. This whole process will take thirty minutes. And then you have to listen to the second English tape for the rest of the thirty minutes. Thus, it is a total of sixty minutes of practice every day, except Sunday.

Seongsil Park: That seems too tight. There is not much time for writing down the explanations of English vocabulary using the

English-English dictionary.

Dr. Peter Lee: Yes, you are right. This process is too tight. You might not have enough time to summarize English vocabulary in your English notes. Making a summary of English vocabulary is extra work for learners who hope to enhance their English writing skills. However, about an hour every day except Sunday is enough time for you to increase your listening, speaking, reading, and writing skills.

Seongsil Park: I see. Now, I know that I have to spend an hour a day during the week. For the first tape, I have to spend an hour listening to it. But when I start to take dictation of it, I can listen to only thirty minutes of the second English tape.

Dr. Peter Lee: However, you will listen to the English tape while taking dictation as well.

Seongsil Park: Yes, you are right. On the basis of your instruction, I am going to spend about forty minutes on listening practice.

Dr. Peter Lee: Yes, you are right. In learning English, listening practice is more important than speaking, reading, and writing. The increase of the percentage of the public English listening tests is the evidence of the importance of English listening.

Seongsil Park: Do you think that the percentage of English listening tests will increase even more?

Dr. Peter Lee: Yes, definitely. I will give you a question to help you understand the reason. Do you agree with this statement: If you listen to English conversations more, you can speak English better. If yes, please tell me why?

Seongsil Park: I don't know.

Dr. Peter Lee: If you listen to the sound of English correctly, your pronunciation will improve dramatically. There is a logical reason for this. If you listen to the sound of English correctly, it means that you can distinguish some confusing sounds such as the R sound and L sound. Of course, those two sounds are totally different from each other. However, many Korean students cannot distinguish an R sound from an L sound because there is no L sound in Korean.

Seongsil Park: Yes, you are right. In Korean, there is no L sound.

Dr. Peter Lee: Why don't you read this sentence aloud?

*Your regular English speaking practice has resulted in your becoming a good English speaker.*

Students in the class: (Altogether) *Your regular English speaking practice has resulted in your becoming a good English speaker.*

Dr. Peter Lee: Okay, very good! However, some of you are still confused between the R sound and L sound. The word that you have to be careful to pronounce is RESULT. Some students pronounced it as RESURT. If you said RESURT, it seems that you are pronouncing the word RESORT. A RESORT is a place for rest and recreation. That is why native English speakers cannot understand what you are talking about.

Somang Kim: So what do I have to do in order to pronounce English words correctly?

Dr. Peter Lee: You have to listen to English carefully. If you listen to the sound of English well, it will be easy for you to distinguish similar sounds. If you listen to English well, your pronunciation will change dramatically because you will know that your old pronunciation is wrong. When you can pronounce the sounds of English correctly, it means that you can listen to all the sounds of English correctly as well. Do you understand what I mean?

Somang Kim: Yes, I understand, and now I know why you are continually emphasizing the importance of English listening practice.

Dr. Peter Lee: Many people go to English countries to learn English. I don't want to stop them doing this because that is their decision. I am sure they think about how much money they have to spend during their stay in an English country. They may also be sad that they have to live separately from their families for a while. I really don't want to stop them because they may be prepared for all these obstacles. However, there is only one thing that I really want to say to them.

Somang Kim: What is that?

Dr. Peter Lee: If parents want to send children to an English country, please train them to listen to English for one or two years before they leave. If students want to learn English in an English country, please listen to English for one or two years before they go. If students have not listened to English since they started learning English, please don't allow them to participate in English programs abroad. They should do English listening practice for one or two years before they go.

Somang Kim: Why do you want to stop them going abroad?

Dr. Peter Lee: Because they will regret it if they don't do English listening practice. Do you know how many students fail in learning English abroad? Some students who have learned English in an English country might say that they learned so many things such as culture and lifestyle. However, their main objective in going abroad is to LEARN ENGLISH. I think that it would be good to learn different cultures, ways of thinking, and lifestyles. However, I really don't want them to waste their money and savings on something they are not prepared for.

Somang Kim: Do you think that they waste their money while learning English in an English country?

Dr. Peter Lee: No, that is not what I mean. I am just worried that some of them might regret their decision after realizing that they wasted their time, money, and effort.

If they had listened to English for several years in Korea, they could've obtained much greater success from attending English programs abroad.

If parents had taught their children English listening practice for several years before sending them abroad, they could've saved a lot of money. Do you know that many students who have participated in English programs abroad realize the importance of English listening practice? After they studied in English programs abroad, they regretted not doing English listening practice. What if they did English listening practice before they attended English programs abroad? Their English ability could've been dramatically improved. They could improve their English ability much faster than others who regarded English listening practice as unimportant.

I have always emphasized that English listening practice is the most important process that you must take in order to learn English fast.

Somang Kim: I must remember this!

Dr. Peter Lee: One more thing! What is the shortcut to learning English?

Students in the class: (Altogether) Listening!

Dr. Peter Lee: Yes, you are right. The shortcut to learning English is listening. You must remember this at all times.

Students in the class: (Altogether) Yes. We must always remember it.

Dr. Peter Lee: Yes, I am proud that all of you here are very smart. If you are spending an hour every day, except Sunday, following my instructions, you can use English well.

Somang Kim: When can I use English well?

Dr. Peter Lee: I cannot guarantee the exact time that you can speak English well. However, there should be no one who can stop you from learning English. Do you know why?

Somang Kim: I don't know.

Dr. Peter Lee: Because you will be very confident when you keep learning English according to my instructions. The first English tape that you choose may not be easy for you because you have to take dictation of it. However, you will feel more confident when you finish it.

When you finish the second tape, you will be more confident going through the process. In order to finish the third tape, you won't need to listen to it a hundred times because you can understand it well even before listening to it a hundred times. You will feel the same thing when you finish the fourth, fifth, and sixth tape.

Somang Kim: Really?

Dr. Peter Lee: Even though the degree of difficulty of the latter English tapes may be higher, the time to complete them may decrease. This suggests that your English ability may be improving as time goes by. Your English listening skill will be much better than before because you have been exposed repeatedly to the entire process of listening. Do you know what this is called?

Somang Kim: Do you call this improvement?

Dr. Peter Lee: That is called PROGRESS in learning English.

You can identify that learning English is much easier than before as you listen to English well. It is therefore important to choose carefully the kind of English listening environments you are exposed to.

Somang Kim: What about speaking?

Dr. Peter Lee: In the beginning, you could not speak English well. Let us think about how babies start to speak. They just cry when they are born. They don't know their language. However, as they get older, they learn a language from their parents and people around them. They can say 'mama' or 'papa' when they are one or two years old. When they are three or four years old, they may be saying some short phrases or sentences. And when they become elementary school students, they start speaking in some more structured sentences. When they are middle school students, they can speak their language without any difficulty. Your English speaking ability will gradually improve in the manner I described above.

Somang Kim: Really?

Dr. Peter Lee: Languages are different from each other but the manner of learning languages is the same. Someone might feel difficulty saying even one or two English words even though they have studied English for more than ten years. However, don't worry about that. It is not true that you are not good at speaking English. It is true that you are not good at speaking English for now because you have never practiced English speaking! If you listen to English tapes and if you read English sentences aloud every day, you can speak English well. At the beginning, your speaking is like the following sentences.

Hi.... My name is... Peter Lee... My hobby is....watching... TV. My....favorite drama is....

Do you know what I mean? In the beginning you may hesitate about what to say and how to say it in English. However, that is the same process that every language learner goes through while learning a language. That is why you don't need to worry about speaking English. If you keep listening to English tapes and reading aloud what you wrote after the dictation, you will, all of a sudden, start to speak good English. In the beginning, your English sentences will be very short. However, you will make very long sentences which are very well-organized in the future, if you keep taking English speaking practice.

Somang Kim: That is the goal that I really want to achieve. I have failed several times in learning English. I don't know whether I have to follow your method and instruction or not.

Dr. Peter Lee: You need just three to six months. I don't want to say that you have to follow others who took several years to learn English. I also don't have much time to focus only on teaching you. However, I would really like to advise you to follow my instructions on the correct way of learning English for three to a maximum of six months. After that period of time, you can recognize whether my instruction is right or wrong. But there is one condition.

Somang Kim: What is that?

Dr. Peter Lee: You must keep following my rules for three to six months. Some students used to break my rules and change my method without consulting me. When you realize that my method is right, you will never stop learning English because you will be very confident about what you are doing to learn English. There is no one who can stop you because you absolutely believe that the way you are learning English is the right path, which is less travelled by many English learners or those of any other nationality. However, it has made all the difference in learning English.

# 9

## Talent, Direction, Methods, and Dreams

Somang Kim: Actually, I gave up learning English since I graduated from high school. While learning English at school, it was so difficult to understand English grammar and other things. In addition, I couldn't guess how long I had to learn English if I wanted to become a good English user. Even if I had studied English for several years, I couldn't speak even short English sentences in front of foreigners. That is why I abandoned learning English. I still have doubts about whether your method will work for me or not.

Dr. Peter Lee: You need the courage to decide on whether you will follow my instructions or not. You must also keep following the rules of learning English that I made. I don't want to push you to follow my instructions. However, I really would like all of my students here to try my method for only three to six months. I know that your time is very valuable, just like your life. I always think that you have a lot of potential and you need to draw it out. Do you have a dream?

Somang Kim: Yes, I have.

Dr. Peter Lee: What is your dream?

Somang Kim: My dream is to become a leader in the tourism and hospitality industry.

Dr. Peter Lee: Can you tell me more specifically the role you would like?

Somang Kim: I would like to be an owner of a franchise in the hotel and restaurant industry.

Dr. Peter Lee: Then, why do you want to learn English?

Somang Kim: If I work in a hotel or restaurant, I will meet many foreigners. I may talk to them when they need some help. Thus, English is one good communication tool for people to interact with each other. Additionally, in order to manage hotel or restaurant franchises, not only in Korea but also in the world, I need professional English ability to communicate with people.

Dr. Peter Lee: That is such a great dream! I definitely believe that you will achieve your dream some day if you have faith. However, you need to make an effort to accomplish your dream. You know this sentence that we discussed a while ago, "No pain, no gain." This means that you have to study English REALLY hard.

Somang Kim: That is right. Everybody knows that.

Dr. Peter Lee: You are right. Everybody knows that. But you know too that there are not many people who achieve their dream. Do you know why?

Somang Kim: I don't know.

Dr. Peter Lee: You need to know how and where you will make an effort. In addition, you need to know that you have to make an effort with something special.

Somang Kim: What is that?

Dr. Peter Lee: There is not one unique answer. But there is a possible answer which is not too far from everyone's opinion. I know that you are a really good student. Not only you but also the other students here have a lot of potential. You will become good leaders in the future. I am SURE that you will become a good leader. However, you need to know something special inside you.

Somang Kim: What is that?

Dr. Peter Lee: Your unique talent!

Somang Kim: My unique talent?

Dr. Peter Lee: Yes, your unique talent! You need to know what your unique talent is. You have to develop your ability on the basis of your unique talent.

Somang Kim: I don't know what my unique talent is.

Dr. Peter Lee: That is why you need to try to find it out. I think that, sometimes, the saddest thing is that people die without knowing their talent. I cannot say many things here in this English class so I want to say only one thing pertinent to English. All students here have their unique talents and their talent could be more fruitful when it is combined with English ability. I don't want all of you here to become English teachers. But I really hope that you will use English well in the field where you are working. Using another language well gives you the power to achieve your goal. It is a priority. If you can use English well, you can communicate with people all over the world. It means that you can get a job not only in Korea but also in the world. As you know, Korea is a small country and it is really tough to get a job in Korea. Competition is very strong. However, if you can use English well, you will have a lot of opportunities to get a job around the world. Have you ever imagined working with foreigners in many different countries? One day, you are working in the United States of America and, in another day, you are working in Switzerland. One day, you will be having lunch, and reading a newspaper in a café in Paris. Please close your eyes and imagine whatever you want.

Somang Kim: It is so great! But could it be possible?

Dr. Peter Lee: Yes, of course. Your dream will definitely come true if you always have faith toward your dream. Every day, you have to say to yourself:

I CAN DO IT! I CAN DO IT! I CAN DO IT!

Do you know that a dream is an extremely powerful way to make your life hopeful and fruitful? You don't spend any money when you are dreaming. But you need to make an effort.

Somang Kim: You are right. But how and where should I make

an effort?

Dr. Peter Lee: You need to know your TALENT, DIRECTION, and METHOD to make your dream come true.

I mentioned earlier that using English well is an advantage getting a job in the world. I also expect you to use English as a tool to make yourself competitive. Do you think that English is difficult?

Somang Kim: Yes, it is difficult.

Dr. Peter Lee: You may be right. Even if learning English is difficult, please believe that using good English is important and will lead you to succeed. That is why you try to learn English. English is an international language so that many people in the world use it. You will realize how important English ability is in the workplace. That is why I really hope you to take up the challenge again to learn English.

Somang Kim: I really want to speak English well. But I don't know what I should do.

Dr. Peter Lee: If you know your talent, then you need to know a specific direction that you can further improve your talent. I mean, the right direction is one which can make your dream come true. I don't know what your dream is but I do know how to learn English. If you can use English well, the length of time that you have to wait for your dream to be accomplished is much shorter. Your dream will become a reality, not just a dream. I am sure that you will be very competitive if you can use English well. That is why I am trying to lead you into the right way to learn English through this lecture.

I mentioned earlier that in Hebrew the meaning of education is repetition. Thus, I am going to make a summary of how to correctly learn English. We discussed the right and wrong methods of learning English in the first part of this class. Do you know why?

Somang Kim: Yes, I do. We tried to distinguish the right methods of learning English from the wrong methods through a lot of discussion.

Dr. Peter Lee: You are right. We recognized bad, useless, unpleasant, and even harmful ways of learning English through a lot of discussion. I really hope that you are no longer following a wrong way of learning English. In addition, please remember the different ways of learning English as suggested by your classmates. Of course, continue to study them carefully. I don't want to explain repeatedly bad and harmful methods of learning English.

Before wrapping up this class, I want to emphasize the correct way of learning English again. If you miss some important points or recommendations for learning English which we discussed earlier, please remember carefully the following seven rules!

# 10

## Seven rules of English learning activities

Somang Kim: Seven rules?

Dr. Peter Lee: Yes, seven rules. While learning English you must follow the seven rules that I am going to tell you, without breaking any of them. Please promise to keep the following rules that I am going to review. If you want to change the rules, please do it after following all the rules completely for three to six months. Do you promise?

Students in the class: (Altogether) Yes, we promise.

Dr. Peter Lee: Okay. Listen carefully. The FIRST RULE that you must follow is to select the right English tape of which you can understand seventy percent. If you are a beginner at learning English, don't select a difficult tape such as English news or movies because the people there speak very fast and use a combination of difficult words and expressions. It would be good for beginners to choose an English tape with a simple dialogue expressed in simple words. If you want to make good conversations in English, you need to select a good tape of an English dialogue. If you want to speak just like a news anchor, you select a tape containing a news anchor's dialogue. However, I really recommend you start this listening process with an English conversation tape. Please remember that you must start to learn English from the right starting point. The right starting point of learning English is to choose an English tape which is suited for your level. Will you do that?

Students in the class: (Altogether) Yes, we will!

Dr. Peter Lee: Alright! The SECOND RULE that you must follow in learning English is to listen regularly to the English tape that you selected. Please listen to it once or twice per day with full attention. If you listen to it walking down the street, riding a bicycle, or getting on a bus, it is not listening but just hearing. You must focus on listening to it at least once a day. Will you do that?

Students in the class: (Altogether) Yes, we will!

Dr. Peter Lee: The THIRD RULE that you must follow is to listen to the first English tape that you selected from beginning to end, more than a hundred times. Don't say that listening twenty or thirty times would be enough for you! You must listen to the whole content of the first English tape a hundred times.

MORE THAN A HUNDRED TIMES!

You must remember and believe that listening to one English tape more than a hundred times is the process for establishing a good English ground in your brain. If you keep following this rule, I am sure that you will speak English very fluently in the future.

Many Koreans translate Korean sentences into English ones before speaking English. They make an English sentence after thinking about its Korean equivalent. They try to translate Korean sentences into English sentences. That is why the sentence that they come up with is called *Konglish*, which means English sentences spoken or written in a Korean way. That is a symptom that many Koreans have in their spoken and written English because they underestimate English listening practice.

If you listen to an English tape more than a hundred times, you can use a lot of English sentences in it without difficulty. As you accumulate more English tapes that you listen to, each more than a hundred times, you can speak English very fluently without undergoing the translating process that many Korean people do. You can speak English in English ways, not in Korean ways. English sentences will be fluently and automatically spoken from your mouth. Will you do that?

Students in the class: (Altogether) Yes, we will!

Dr. Peter Lee: The FOURTH RULE that you must follow is to take dictation of the English tapes that you have listened to more than a hundred times.

Don't take dictation on an English tape to which you have listened less than a hundred times. Students may take dictation after listening to it only once because they think that they can understand everything spoken in it already. No way!

Taking dictation of English tapes to which you have listened more than a hundred times is an extremely important process for matching the sounds of English that you listen to and the letters of English that you write.

You must also remember that taking dictation is a way to match the sound and letter of spoken English. That is why you must go through this process even though it is not easy. Many students usually give up this process because they think that it is too difficult. However, you have to overcome this difficulty in order to further learn English on the right track. Will you do that?

Students in the class: (Altogether) Yes, we will!

Dr. Peter Lee: The FIFTH RULE that you must follow is to take dictation of five or six English tapes.

Taking dictation of one or two English tapes wouldn't be enough for you to distinguish precisely all the sounds of English. In addition, you couldn't listen to all of the sounds of English correctly after doing only one or two English tapes. Based on my previous experience, I think that five or six tapes are enough to be proficient with English sounds. And you don't need to take dictation of all English tapes because you can correctly and precisely listen to all English sounds after taking dictation of five or six English tapes.

If you feel that you need to train your ears more, please take dictation of more English tapes. However, as I said, you don't need to take dictation of every English tape. You need to manage your time for learning English. This means that you need to keep studying English until the time that you feel you don't need to take dictation anymore.

For example, you took dictation of Korean when you were an elementary school student. Nobody takes dictation of Korean when already in middle or high school. Do you understand what I mean through this example?

Students in the class: (Altogether) Yes, we do.

Dr. Peter Lee: The SIXTH RULE that you must follow is to take dictation of an English tape for fifteen minutes per day. Please take dictation on whatever portion of an English tape you can read aloud for fifteen minutes. You must read English aloud EVERYDAY if you want to speak English well.

Do you want to speak English well? You must take time to practice speaking. How to practice? Read the dictated paper aloud that you did daily! This is a very simple answer for how to speak English well. If you want to speak English well, please READ English sentences aloud EVERYDAY!

Many English learners never read English aloud and they always analyze the structure of English sentences. They always think that they are the best when they know English grammar better than others, even though native English speakers never consider English grammar as the main ingredient in English proficiency. Please read English sentences aloud if you want to speak English well.

Some English learners complain that they could be good English speakers if they learned English in English countries. That is why they are always bothering their parents to attend English programs in English countries which are very expensive. They always complain about their environment. But the most important thing is not to mind those obstacles in learning English. Don't complain about where you are! You must deal with your circumstances and overcome any obstacles. How? Let me tell you some methods for dealing with any barriers that interrupt your determination of learning English, and how to overcome them.

There are many situations that knock down your determination in learning English. What if you don't have enough money to attend English programs in English countries? What if your parents cannot support you to attend English programs in English countries? What if you don't have an English friend in Korea? Then, please talk to your Korean friends in English. Don't laugh at me! Why not talk to your Korean friends in English? Of course, I am not saying that you should always talk to your Korean friends in English even if you are with other Korean friends. I strongly recommend that you need to meet with them regularly to discuss matters in English. I also did that when I was young. I met my Korean friends to talk in English for one or two hours everyday. It worked. It really worked! I definitely believe that *Konglish* will become English eventually.

One must realize that nobody can speak English perfectly when they are a beginner. Did you speak Korean perfectly when you were young? No way! Don't worry about your English sentences! Please try to speak English even if you are not a good English speaker yet. I definitely believe that you will be much better than some English learners who always hesitate to speak English. They always think that they need time to perfect their English ability. The time that they make their English ability perfect may come very late or may not come at all if they don't strive hard. Thus, please take dictation of English tapes and read dictated papers aloud every day. Of course, while reading them aloud you must always think about the correct pronunciation, accent, and intonation that you listened to on the tapes. The reason that you must listen to it a hundred times is to make your intonation, accent, and pronunciation just like that of native English speakers.

It is actually very easy to know whether you have listened to an English tape a hundred times or not. Do you know how this is done? If I let students read their dictated papers aloud, then I can guess who listened to it a hundred times. The person who follows exactly its intonation, accent, and pronunciation is the one who listened to it a hundred times. Please listen a hundred times to each English tape that you choose, take dictation of it, and read the dictated paper aloud. This is the right process for you to practice English from listening skills to speaking skills. Trust me! Will you do that?

Students in the class: (Altogether) Yes, we will!

Dr. Peter Lee: The SEVENTH RULE that you must follow is to take a rest on Sunday.

Don't listen to any English tape to which you have listened regularly during the week. I will explain why you need to take a rest on Sunday.

If you work every day without resting, would it be good for your health? Of course not! If you listen to an English tape, that is also work. Your brain absolutely needs a REST. This means that your brain needs time to arrange all of the English information gained during weekdays into the English ground of your brain.

There is one important thing that you can experience after taking a rest on Sunday. That is the evidence that you are progressing daily in learning English. While listening to the English tape that you chose at the beginning, you couldn't perceive all the sounds spoken. However, as time goes by, you will observe that you can now listen to some sounds to which you couldn't listen the previous week, right after taking a rest on Sunday. For example, you failed to perceive the sounds of *R, L, TH,* and *V* because you had never listened to them before. In addition, you may not know the difference between the *S* sound and the *TH* sound if you have never heard of those sounds before. However, as you listen to the English tapes regularly, you can distinguish the sound differences between *S* and *TH, D* and *T, F* and *V*, and other similar sounds. If you want to improve your English listening skill and if you want to be able to distinguish all the letters in English, you need to listen to English tapes regularly. If you expect this experience after listening only one or two times, it will be WRONG!

As I said earlier, you must listen to one English tape a hundred times. If you listen to it twice per day, it will take about one and a half months. During that time, you will rest every Sunday. After resting on Sunday, you should be able to listen to *L, V, TH,* and other sounds which you hardly heard in the past. You can listen to English better after taking a rest on Sunday. This is the reason why resting is extremely important.

As a matter of fact, you can improve your English as you listen to English tapes more frequently. That is truth that everyone should know. Thus, listening to your selected English tape more frequently is enough evidence that you are progressing in English listening skill. This progress helps you to continually learn English without pausing or giving up. If your listening ability is better than before, you realize that you are more confident than before, because you can listen to English better. That will make you satisfied and nobody will be able to make you stop learning because you will be very confident about what you are doing to learn English.

I am sure that you have heard people's success stories through books or newspapers. Some people demonstrate their success on television programs and you may be very impressed. Don't envy them because I believe that you will become a successful person in the future. Please be successful in learning English, so that you will be the envy of everyone!

You will be successful in learning English if you keep following the rules that I taught you. At least you will listen to English well and speak it very fluently if you just follow all of these seven rules. You don't need a lot of money to listen and speak English well. You only need around five dollars to buy one English tape.

Some students here might think that listening to one English tape is absolutely not enough to improve their listening and speaking skills. Of course! One English tape is not enough for you to become a good English listener and speaker. However, I strongly advise that your first step in learning English is definitely listening to English. Listening is always the first step in learning not only English, but also any other spoken language. In addition, if you can use English well, you can make good conversation. How can you make a good dialogue? First, you definitely must listen to what other people say. I really like this sentence written in the Holy Bible.

*Hear, my son, and be wise! (Proverbs 23:19)*

If you listen first, that is the right way to start a good conversation. If you don't listen to others first, you cannot make a good dialogue. Thus, please LISTEN to all of the seven rules and follow them. Will you do that?

Students in the class: (Altogether) Yes, we will.

Dr. Peter Lee: The following comments are not a rule that you must follow but recommendations which are helpful for you to enhance your English ability.

Please use both the English-Korean dictionary and the English-English dictionary. While listening to an English tape, you may want to know some words in it. Then, please check them using both English dictionaries. If you check out a word using the English-English dictionary, please write down the explanation of it and read it aloud. This is good practice for enhancing your English writing skills.

Anyway, I really want you to follow all of the seven rules which can definitely help you enhance your listening and speaking skills in English. Some students may insist that there are other ways to learn English and listening cannot be the first step in learning English.

However, I strongly insist on the following sentence.

LISTENING IS THE FIRST STEP IN LEARNING ENGLISH!

I definitely believe that there is only one rule which is absolutely correct in learning a spoken language. The first step to learn languages, including English, is LISTENING. This rule has never changed. I am sure everyone definitely agrees with my opinion because they also learned their mother tongue from listening.

Do you want to know the fastest way to learn English or a shortcut for learning English? That is...

LISTENING TO ENGLISH!

Do you want to know how to listen to English? Please follow the seven rules that I shared with you in this class. I guarantee that you will experience something that I have experienced while learning English, if you follow the seven rules that I suggested in this class. I definitely believe that the way we learned our mother tongue is the correct way to learn foreign languages. Therefore, we also need to adapt the way of learning our mother tongue to our English learning process. If you make an effort to learn English using the right way, YOU WILL NEVER FAIL! You may fall down sometimes because learning English is not easy, but rather time-consuming. But you have to use your valuable time for learning English in the right way.

You must follow the first rule of learning every spoken language which is LISTENING. I really want to emphasize one more thing for learning English that you must remember always if you want to learn English.

PLEASE LISTEN AND BE WISE!

Last but not least, I would like to wrap up this class by saying this sentence again, which I mentioned earlier in the lecture. I really believe in this sentence:

*"The tongue has the power of life and death, and those who love it will eat its fruit (Proverbs 18:21)."*

If you say that you can become a good English speaker, then you will DEFINITELY become a good English speaker in the future.

Thank you so much.

GOD bless everyone!

# Conclusion

How do you feel after taking this class? Are you still confused about what you should do to learn English? All the explanations for learning English written in this book are quite straightforward.

In brief, you must learn English the proper way, in exactly the same manner that you learned your mother tongue. You learned your native language from listening. If you learned your native language from speaking, reading, or writing, the sounds you speak in your native language would be totally weird compared to others who have the same mother tongue. If you didn't know the sounds of letters in your mother tongue, you wouldn't know how to speak, read, and write those words and letters. When you listen to the specific sound of words in your mother tongue, then you understand how to speak, read, and write them. If you want to learn English, you must follow the right steps in learning a language. The correct order in learning English language competencies is this: listening, speaking, reading, and writing. There is no way to deny this fact because you learned your mother tongue according to the same steps.

Many people say that learning English is difficult as they learn more and more about it. However, it doesn't make sense because the more they learn about English, the more information about English they discover. If they have more information about English, it means that English should be easier than before.

The fundamental reason why they feel that English is difficult is that the foundation of their English ability is too weak and vulnerable.

Without English listening practice, they studied English grammar!

Without English listening practice, they memorized English words!

Without English listening practice, they spoke poor English!

Without English listening practice, they read English materials!

Without English listening practice, they wrote English sentences!

Without English listening practice, learning English is limited and there is no guarantee in developing English abilities. If you teach English, what learning activity, among listening, speaking, reading, and writing, would you let your students do? If you feel that you failed to learn English because you studied English without considering the correct steps in learning a language, would you still recommend to students to follow the steps you did? I am sure that you would not.

Some learners feel that English listening practice is boring and that it may be hard to measure the improvement in one's English listening ability compared to speaking, reading, and writing abilities. However, English listening practice is the most important activity for constructing the English ground in your brain. Even if the existence of the English ground of the brain is not scientifically proven, it is a repository where you store all the information you learned that pertains to English by listening, speaking, reading, and writing English.

The power of the English ground of the brain is immeasurable. If you have an English ground in your brain, you can receive a lot of English information, including English words and sentences by listening and reading with ease.

However, there is one thing to remember. There is no shortcut to building an English ground in your brain. It takes TIME, just as babies have their own language ground in their brains. When they start to learn how to speak their mother tongue, it takes at least one to two years for them to build the language ground in their brain.

Of course, you need to continually speak, read, and write English while building an English ground in your brain. The point is that it is the correct step to developing one's English ability through listening. Without listening practice, it would be impossible to improve one's English ability.

Another power of the English ground in the brain is that the speed of learning English increases. Without the English ground in the brain, all English vocabulary must be memorized. All the

English words memorized without the English ground in the brain could easily be forgotten because there is no storage area or space for the vocabulary to be kept. The function of the English ground of the brain is to make any English information be stored and remembered in the brain, just like how the brain of a child absorbs the information that he or she receives through listening, watching, and reading.

The following chart shows the speed of English learning methods. There are two cases involved: one represents the way of learning English without English listening practice while the other one represents the way of learning English with English listening practice.

CHART

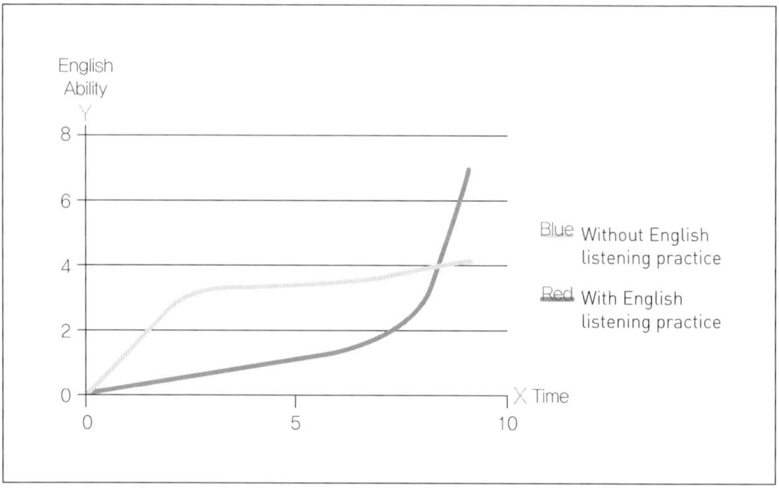

The red line represents the case of learning English with English listening practice while the blue line represents the case of learning English without English listening practice. Axis X represents TIME and axis Y represents English ability. In the case of the blue line, people memorize many English words and read a lot of English materials without any English listening practice. In the case of the red line, people listen to English, memorize a few English words, and read small amounts of English materials because they think that English listening practice is the first step in learning English. At the beginning, people in the blue line seem to know English better than people in the red line. However, the English ability of people in the red line quickly increases by a great deal!

THUS, ENGLISH LISTENING PRACTICE IS THE MOST BASIC AND ESSENTIAL STEP IN DEVELOPING ENGLISH ABILITY. Learning English should be done in the same order as you learned your mother tongue: listening, speaking, reading, and writing.

THIS HAS BEEN PROVEN TO BE TRUE!

**Daehui Peter Lee, Ph.D.**

Assistant Professor at Soonchunhyang University

Received the Bachelor of Arts degree in English Language and Literature at Korea University, Korea; received the Master of Science degree with a major in International Tourism and Hotel Management at Hanyang University, Korea; completed the requirements for the Doctor of Philosophy degree with a major in Hospitality Administration at Oklahoma State University, the United States.